The Journey

Tom Gilligan

Copyright © 2024 by – Tom Gilligan – All Rights Reserved.

It is not legal to reproduce, duplicate, or transmit any part of this document in either electronic means or printed format. Recording of this publication is strictly prohibited.

Contents

Dedication i
Acknowledgement ii
About the Author iii
Prologue 2
Preparation 7
Day (1): 150 Km 10
    July 8th Total 150 Km
Day (2): 105 Km 14
    July 9th Total 255 Km
Day (3): 126 Km 20
    July 10th Total 381 Km
Day (4): 84 Km 25
    July 11th Total 460 Km
Day (5): 114 Km 30
    July 12th Total 563 Km
Day (6): 38 Km 34
    July 13th Total 600 Km
Day (7): 65 Km 37
    July 14th Total 665 Km
Day (8) 125 Km 41
    July 15th Total 790 Km
Day (9): 85 Km 48
    July 16th Total 875 Km
Day (10): 110 Km 50
    July 17th Total 985 Km
Day (11): 40 Km 54

July 18th Total 1025 Km
Day (12): Rest Day..59
July 19th Total 1025 Km
Day (13): 215 Km 61
July 20th Total 1240 Km
Day (14): 60 Km 65
July 21st Total 1300 Km
Day (15): 142 Km 69
July 22nd Total 1442 Km
Day (16): 34 Km 75
July 22nd Total 1476 Km
Day (17): 130 Km 78
July 24th Total 1606 Km
Day (18): 141 Km 81
July 25th Total 1747 Km
Day (19): 93 Km 83
July 26th Total 1840 Km
Day (20): 235 Km 85
July 27th Total 2075 Km
Day (21): 160 Km 88
July 28th Total 2235 Km
Day (22): 168 Km 91
July 28th Total 2403 Km
Day (23): 80 Km 94
July 29th Total 2483 Km
Day (24 -25): REST DAYS 97
July 30th – August 1st Total 2483 Km

Day (26): 100 Km 99
    August 2nd Total 2583 Km
Day (27): 114 Km 101
    Aug 3rd Total 2697 Km
Day (28): 120 Km 105
    August 4th Total 2817 Km
Day (29): 101 Km 107
    August 5th Total 2918 Km
Day (30): 109 Km 108
    August 6th Total 3027 Km
Day (31): 122 Km 110
    August 7th Total 3149 Km
Day (32): 115 Km 113
    August 8th Total 3264 Km
Day (33): REST DAY 117
    August 9th Total 3264 Km
Day (34): 105 Km 120
    August 10th Total 3359 Km
Day (35): 90 Km 123
    August 11th Total 3449 Km
Day (36): 150 Km 125
    August 12th Total 3599 Km
Day (37): 135 Km 132
    August 13th Total 3734 Km
Day (38): 130 Km 135
    August 14th Total 3864 Km
Day (39): REST DAY 140

August 15th Total 3864 Km
Day (40): 160 Km 144
August 16th Total 4024 Km
Day (41): 120 Km 148
August 17th Total 4144 Km
Day (42): 145 Km 151
August 18th Total 4289 Km
Day (43): 110 Km 156
August 19th Total 4399 Km
Day (44): 205 Km 158
August 20th Total 4604 Km
EPILOGUE 164
STATISTICS 168
BRITISH COLUMBIA to MANITOBA 169
MANITOBA to ONTARIO 170

Dedication

To my children, Sean, and Michelle, who will be in my heart forever.

Acknowledgement

To Marg Gilligan, the mother of our children, who met me on the journey.

To John and Susan Razulis for their support and kindness. I will always be grateful to them.

To Diane Green, who worked long into the night to discipline my punctuation, and Betty Schultz, Shelly Green, and Henry Rutgers, who straightened out my syntax: many thanks, dear friends.

To Gordon Davidson and Tina Rochford, for the love and support that enabled me to commence my journey.

To Jaia Friesen, whose magic helped me to find my way home.

To my dear wife, Lucy, for her support and patience, as I finished the journey of writing this story.

About the Author

Tom Gilligan is a retired psychologist. The death of his father precipitated a change in his career from marketing to psychology, a change that required many years as a full-time mature student attending various universities in Canada. During that time, he became separated from his two children. This memoir tells the tale of his solo journey across Canada on a used bicycle to rejoin them. At times he was alone and at risk in a world that had not yet developed such things as cell phones, personal computers, and the internet to facilitate communication. He now lives on a small island off the west coast of British Columbia with his wife and a large dog. He has published articles in professional journals and written many psychological reports about others. This is the first time that he has told his own story, but it won't be his last.

I was 44 when I decided to ride a used bicycle 4,600 kilometres from Vancouver to Toronto. This account of my journey is not intended to advise or guide anyone on how to bicycle across Canada but is simply part of my story, as we all have stories about events and remembered experiences from our lives. Now that I approach the last stage of a much longer journey, I think of my children, grandchildren, and others to come, and hope that in reading this tale, they will come to know something about me and my life.

Prologue

I was driving on the campus grounds of The University of British Columbia when the random action of a stranger changed my life.

The early morning mist had cleared, sunlight was chasing shadows across an empty road, and my day had started well. I stopped to allow an aged couple to cross the road. They smiled at me, stepped off the sidewalk, and then, with a startled look in my direction, hastily stepped back again. And if the driver of the grimy orange truck had been paying attention, instead of bending down to change the channel on his radio, he would not have slammed into the back of my stationary vehicle at 60 kph. The impact destroyed my ancient Plymouth Station Wagon and severely injured my neck, but it also provided the means for me to cycle 4,600 kilometres across Canada from Vancouver to Toronto, and on that journey, I discovered new meaning in my life!

However, I am leaving out significant details and getting ahead of myself in telling this tale!

In April 1984, I was living in Toronto and separated from my wife Marg and my two children: my daughter, Michelle, aged 15, and my son, Sean, aged 10. I had a master's degree in counselling psychology from the University of British Columbia and was employed as a vocational rehabilitation counsellor. At the beginning of the year, I was accepted into the doctoral program in Counselling Psychology at The University of British Columbia, to commence in the fall. I had accepted this offer with mixed feelings. On the one hand I wanted to obtain registration as a psychologist, which required a doctoral degree, however, it also meant I would have to reside in Vancouver and be separated from my children for more than three years.

Eventually, I overcame my misgivings by reasoning that I could periodically return to Toronto to spend time with them or have them spend time with me in Vancouver.

Four months later, in August of 1984, I left Toronto and set off toward Vancouver, 4600 kilometres west along the TransCanada Highway. My good friend, Jack Razulis, accompanied me as we drove my old Plymouth Station Wagon around the Great Lakes, across The Prairies, and over The Rocky Mountains to British Columbia. We camped along the way in provincial parks and commercial campgrounds. Jack stayed for a week in Vancouver and then returned to Toronto. I commenced my doctoral program, and for a while, all went well in a familiar academic setting with a faculty that I knew and trusted, or at least went well until that morning in November.

In the weeks that followed the accident, I could not concentrate on my studies. I became discouraged and felt lost and alone in the world. I was 44 years of age, and the violence of the accident left me feeling more vulnerable and aware of the temporary nature of life. My ambition had taken me away from my children, and I wanted to be with them again. However, when I thought about the obstacles I would have to overcome to rejoin them, they seemed insurmountable.

First, I would have to be accepted into an equivalent graduate program in Toronto. And, even if I successfully achieved that objective, I would still have to cover the costs of transportation and moving my belongings from Vancouver to Toronto. And finally, I would have to find the cash to pay for food and accommodation during the summer months. It seemed impossible for me to find a solution to these obstacles, but I was determined to find a way.

In January 1985, I was accepted into the doctoral program in Applied Psychology at The University of Toronto. How I managed to convince the admissions committee to accept my application is another story. I just know that my determination to be with my children opened closed doors and waived the normal admission procedures. Once the academic year commenced in September, I would then qualify for a student loan to cover the basic costs of food, accommodation, and academic fees. However, I still had to find the money for accommodation and food during the summer months and pay for the transportation of myself and my worldly belongings to Toronto.

In February, I obtained a limited amount of insurance compensation for the loss of my station wagon and the injury to my neck. However, my financial future as a student remained precarious, especially when I considered the costs of setting up a home once I reached Toronto. I remember sitting on the couch in my apartment trying to think of economical ways to make the move, even seeing myself walking to Toronto like some kind of hobo.

And then, in a moment of inspiration, I remembered that I could ride a bike and realized that I could significantly reduce my transportation expenses and living costs during the summer months if I purchased one and cycled to Toronto, camping along the way in a rent-free tent.

I now had a plan that would enable me to return to my children!

Two weeks later, I purchased a used bike (a green "Raleigh Touring Bicycle") that had been offered for sale on the notice board of a local grocery store. I paid $110 for the bike, which I thought was quite expensive but decided that it would not really affect my cash reserves since I would be able to sell it after I reached Toronto. Not knowing too much about current bicycles or what type to look for, I was impressed by the name "Touring," which I thought was exactly the type of bike that would be suitable for me to ride across Canada.

I also purchased assorted items of camping equipment from a local Canadian Tire store: these included a small red bivouac tent, a lightweight sleeping bag, cooking utensils, and sundry items. Based on knowledge of these matters acquired during my brief career as a Boy Scout, I believed that this gear would be sufficient for my needs on this epic journey!

It had been 25 years since I had been on a bicycle, and so it took more than a couple of spins around the block to develop sufficient confidence to ride it in highway traffic. During the next four months, I rode the bike for trips about town and between my apartment and the university campus. From my journey by car the previous year, I knew that I would be climbing steep roads, particularly in the Rockies and around Lake Superior. And so, believing that bike technology might compensate for my limited experience in peddling bicycles up the side of mountains, I engaged the services of a local bike shop to change the gears on the bike to those more suited for mountain climbing.

I was active and physically fit for my age, but I knew that I had to prepare for very demanding days, as I cycled such a great distance. I decided that my best strategy would be to gradually develop strength and endurance before leaving Vancouver, by using the bike for all my transportation needs. I also anticipated that my endurance and strength would naturally improve as the journey progressed. Once on the road, I planned to eat at roadside restaurants during the day and pick up bread rolls, fruit, and canned food to heat on a campfire for my evening meals. I had no doubt that I would be successful in this adventure. I had been a first-class Boy Scout in my youth, which meant that I could light a fire on a rock in the middle of a stream with one match and no paper. And so, with that qualification in mind, I felt quite confident that I could camp and bike my way across Canada!

I now had a plan to be with my children again, a plan that included riding a used bicycle from Vancouver to Toronto. However, this immense journey, was one that I could not have afforded, or imagined I would be making, if I had not obtained the unwitting assistance of the young man, who had driven his truck into the back of my station wagon on that fateful November morning! Due to that accident, I became more conscious of the fragility of my life and the pain of being separated from my children, and the compensation cash helped me to return to them. At the time, I remember being quite annoyed with that young man and his carelessness, but in later years I came to appreciate the positive value and lasting change that it brought into my life.

Preparation

Prepared to Leave.

During the week prior to leaving Vancouver, I carefully packed all my belongings, including books and clothing, into eleven boxes, with a combined weight of 460 pounds, and mailed them to my friends in Toronto via Canada Post for $121. The Canada Post rates for shipping boxes were cheaper than any other method of shipment, enabling me to save a significant amount of cash.

To relieve the boredom of endless hours and days of cycling that I imagined, I would face during such a long trip, I packed a CD player and five music cassette tapes, ranging from Beethoven and Dvorak to The Gypsy Kings, The Rolling Stones, and the Motown sound of Diana Ross and The Supremes. A friend gave me an old Minolta 35 mm film camera, which I hoped would take amazing photographs of my epic journey – once I learned how to use it! I also packed a small notebook to record the details of each day on the road and any random thoughts that might occur to me on the way.

I did not want to start my journey by cycling through the fumes and noise of the heavy morning traffic coming into Vancouver, so my friends Gordon and Tina kindly agreed to let me stay overnight with them on Sunday night, and then drive me to Coquitlam (30 kilometres beyond Vancouver) the following morning.

Early, on Sunday morning, I phoned my children in Toronto and talked about the distance and how long it would take me to reach them. Earlier in the month, I sent them a large map of Canada and a box of coloured pins. I told them that I would send postcards and sometimes phone them so they would know where to stick the pins on the map to follow my progress. I told them I loved them and that we would be together soon.

Later in the afternoon, I attached the panniers, containing spare shoes, clothing for different temperature conditions, rain gear, bike tools, and miscellaneous items, to the front and rear of the bike. The tent, sleeping bag, groundsheet, bike, and my good self, weighed in at 250 pounds. It did not occur to me that I would face a significant challenge attempting to carry this weight over the Rocky Mountains, which said something about my determined optimism or mental health at the time!

And so, with a fond farewell to the basement apartment that had been my home for the previous 10 months, I set off down the back alley on the first stage of the immense journey that lay ahead. I felt excited and confident as the bike began to speed up across the rough dirt surface of the alley. However, my enthusiasm did not last. Somewhere around the 50-yard mark, the bike fell over, and I fell off!

Due to my inexperience and limited knowledge concerning bike packing, I had put too much weight onto the front panniers, which prevented the front wheel from turning and caused the bike to fall over. Feeling deflated but relieved that no one had witnessed this sad start to my adventure, I returned to the apartment lawn, repacked, and, in possession of a more balanced understanding of how to pack bike panniers, set out once more to stay with my friends.

Day (1): 150 Km

July 8th
Total 150 Km

Vancouver to The Fraser River Valley

The day began with a large breakfast, heavily loaded with carbohydrates, that, according to my research on the subject, was the essential food for any long-distance bike rider. We sat and talked for a while before I said goodbye to Tina, loaded the bike and panniers into Gordon's car, and the great journey commenced.

The weather was cool and overcast, with a light wind coming from the west. Heavy morning traffic was already streaming down the six-lane highway into Vancouver. We arrived in Coquitlam, 30 kilometres beyond Vancouver, around 8:00 a.m., pulled over to the hard shoulder of the road, unloaded the bike and gear, and then stood quietly talking and observing the traffic going into Vancouver. I remember feeling calm and detached, but my heart was racing, and I was excited to be finally off on the greatest journey of my life. We said goodbye, and I watched Gordon's car disappear into the traffic before turning to my bike and equipment lying in the grass beside me.

Suddenly, I stopped breathing, and a cold panic filled my stomach. Something was wrong! I looked at the ground and saw that the tent and sleeping bag were missing. Distracted by the excitement of leaving, I had left them on the lawn outside Gordon's house back in Vancouver!

I stood by the side of that busy highway, feeling confused and defeated. I had no means of contacting either Gordon or Tina to help me. I remember sitting down on the grass beside the bike, sitting in silence, deaf to the noise of passing traffic and paralyzed by churning thoughts and emotions – a sarcastic sneering voice in my head telling me that I had failed and that my journey was over. I do not know how long I sat there with tears in my eyes, not knowing what to do or how to respond to this disaster. I thought of cycling back into Vancouver to retrieve the tent and sleeping bag but felt so defeated that I could not imagine being able to do it. My sense of despair began to grow stronger. I had given up my apartment and had no where to live except in that tent. I could not go forward and I could not return.

But then I thought of my children, who were waiting for me in Toronto, and with that thought, I stood up, strapped my gear onto the bike, and joined the mindless flow of commuter traffic heading back into Vancouver.

I felt nauseous. My arms were trembling, and I was afraid and. disappointed in myself for making such a stupid mistake. Somewhere along the road back to Vancouver, I concluded that if I could surmount this challenge, then I would be able to cope with any challenges in the days and weeks ahead. I tried to imagine what feelings I might have and where and when I would be in three weeks, but it seemed too far away. And so, I just kept my head down, blanked out the traffic noise and fumes, stopped thinking, and just kept riding; unfortunately, going in the wrong direction!

I reached Gordon's house and found the tent and sleeping bag lying in the open beside the fence, where I had left them. Slowly and carefully, I fastened the equipment onto the bike panniers and, with a renewed determination and sense of purpose, set off to fight the traffic again; this time heading east along The TransCanada Highway toward Toronto.

The excitement and anticipation I had experienced that morning were gone. I only knew that I wanted to escape. I felt pursued and wanted to run like a frightened animal. I felt pursued by my own thoughts and fears of failure if I did not get far away from Vancouver on my first day.

I kept my head down, chanting a mantra to calm my mind, each push of my legs carrying me further down the road and deeper into my journey. I have no memory of the first hour or so after I left Gordon's house, but shortly after noon, I passed the spot where we had said goodbye and felt a deep sense of relief, as though I had just woken up from a bad dream to start a new day. I continued to ride for another hour in what seemed like a trance, before pulling over to the side of the road, where I pushed the bike behind a clump of thick bushes and collapsed on top of my sleeping bag; and there I slept, for an hour, concealed from passing traffic.

Later in the afternoon, I woke to see afternoon sunlight filtering through the leaves above my head. I heard the rumble of heavy traffic coming from the highway and the sound of birds singing in the trees overhead. I felt thirsty and confused. I did not know where I was or why I was lying on the ground, and then I remembered how I got there, where I was going, and the purpose of my journey. And, with that thought, I got back on the bike and set off again, pedalling down the road to Toronto. After half an hour of steady cycling, I found a service station where I purchased canned soup and raisin buns before checking into a small campground beside the highway.

I paid my camping fee at the entrance, and then carefully picked out a campsite near a railway line, away from the other campers and their camper vans, where I set up my tent, before collecting small twigs and branches to make a fire. I boiled water to make tea and heat a can of soup for my evening meal, and then, feeling exhausted, climbed into my sleeping bag and fell asleep.

Suddenly I woke to the sound of a shrill, buzzing, whining noise. In the dim light of the fading day, I perceived a veritable squadron of mosquitoes swirling above my head in an obvious state of excitement, no doubt induced by my plump and edible presence in the tent! Defeated by overwhelming odds, I covered my head inside the sleeping bag and went back to sleep.

At 1:00 a.m., I woke again, this time to the sound of a small tractor circling my secluded campsite, spraying clouds of pungent insecticide; no doubt meant to kill the mosquitoes but including me as collateral damage. I considered clambering out of the tent to make a strong complaint, but I was naked, vulnerable, tired, and alone in the darkness. So, I buried my head deeper into the sleeping bag, surrendered to my cruel fate, and fell asleep, hoping that day two would be an improvement on day one!

Day (2): 105 Km

July 9th
Total 255 Km

Fraser River Valley to Boston Bar

I woke early, packed up the tent and gear and quietly left the silent campground. I had coped with my fear of defeat and failure during the hard ride back into Vancouver, and despite ravenous mosquitoes and pesticide spray, I had been able to sleep my first night outdoors. I had cycled 150 kilometres, more than I had ever done in one day, and was looking forward to my first breakfast on the road.

Fraser River Valley

In sharp contrast to the anxiety and confusion of my first day, I remember feeling calm and aware of my surroundings, as I cycled along the side of the wide and slow-flowing Fraser River. The road was gentle and easy to ride, and I stopped for breakfast in Agassiz, 4 kilometres past the campground, and later purchased food for my lunch and evening meal at a roadside convenience store. I paid $15 for my food supplies and became concerned that I may have underestimated the cost of the food I would have to purchase during this long journey. However, the thought that I would live in a tent and pay no rent, eased my cash concerns.

Later in the morning, the river valley narrowed, the distant mountains came closer, and I climbed my first steep sections of the journey. At the top of each climb, I stood panting for breath and wondered if I would be able to meet the physical and mental challenges of The Rocky Mountains that I knew lay ahead.

Around 1:30 p.m. I arrived at Spuzzum, located in the lower reaches of The Fraser Canyon. The cycling had been difficult and demanding, and I began to doubt the wisdom of the conditioning strategy that I had adopted for the trip. It occurred to me, as I stopped to catch my breath every half hour or so, that my plan to build up strength and endurance on the road, had underestimated the amount of pain and discomfort that would be involved in the first stages of the journey. I had intended to cycle another 60 kilometres and camp at Boston Bar. But I knew that the town was situated at the far end of a much steeper and more difficult section of the canyon, and I was already tired.

And so, I decided to find a local campground off the main highway to spend the night and then attack the deep canyon tomorrow. But after half an hour of fruitless searching for a suitable campground, I gave up and found a quiet glade in the forest, where I sat in the shade of a huge maple tree and ate cold meat buns and fruit for lunch. I then carefully considered my options and reached a decision. Unless I wanted to sleep alone in a forest, inhabited by bears and other large carnivorous animals, I had to face the challenge of riding another 60 kilometres through the deep canyon to Boston Bar, and I had to do it today!

The Fraser Canyon

At first, the ride through the canyon was not as demanding as I had expected, and I stopped at a couple of lookout points, crammed with parked cars and crowds of jostling tourists peering down into the river's rushing waters far below. I watched from a distance. I was curious to see and experience the violent energy of the mighty Fraser River as it smashed against the canyon's walls. But I felt alienated from these jolly crowds of people and wanted no part of their world.

Between Yale and Boston Bar, I came to the first of the seven tunnels of The Fraser Canyon Valley. I stopped before the first tunnel entrance and observed the heavy semi-trailer trucks entering and exiting the gaping tunnel mouth. I could see a railing and narrow path for cyclists or pedestrians. The pathway left little room to ride the bike, especially with the tent and bedding hanging over the side. Eventually, I decided it would be too risky to ride through the tunnel, and so I slowly ventured in, pushing the bike and holding my breath every time a truck roared past, blasting stale air, gritty dust, and diesel fumes into my face. I repeated this performance for the next two tunnels, each time trudging along the narrow bike path and flinching each time a monster truck roared by spewing its foul diesel breath into my face.

When I reached the third tunnel, I noticed that the pedestrian pathway seemed wider than the other tunnels, and I was becoming bored, just plodding along, inhaling fumes, and taking forever to get to the exit. I sat by the entrance to the tunnel and observed the trucks. After watching for ten minutes, I noticed a considerable time gap between each passing truck and wondered if I could ride quickly through the tunnel instead of having to trudge along the pathway pushing the bike.

I remember feeling extremely nervous as I approached the entrance, and wondered if I was risking my life merely to avoid inhaling a few diesel fumes. However, I decided that it had to be safe because I had not seen a warning notice prohibiting cyclists from riding on the pathway. And so, encouraged by my astute thinking on the subject, I left the sanity of the open road and entered the Alexandra Tunnel.

The Alexandra Tunnel

I remember the dim light, stale air, and bitter yellow exhaust fumes that choked my breathing. I felt the fear in my body forcing my legs to pound hard upon the pedals. Eyes tight fixed on the gritted surface of the narrow pathway, strewn with rocks and discarded waste from passing cars, into the tunnel of death rode the brave hero!

I remember the roar of trucks in the darkness coming up behind me, becoming louder and louder. I was confused by the lights blazing, passing close, no margin for error. I was balanced between life and death. A voice in my head demanding that I must not think –stop thinking! Suddenly, I see a small circle of light in the distance, and I pedal like a maniac toward the light, flying out of the darkness and into daylight; I breathe clean air, sunlight on green leaves, birds singing; life rejoined; I am safe once more!

By the time I reached the last and longest of the tunnels, I had mastered the technique of "tunnel bike riding" and, instead of relying on manic energy to propel the bike along the pathway, I could now ride through the tunnel at a steady, confident speed, holding my nerve whenever a truck passed by too close for comfort.

With the last of the tunnels behind me, I continued toward Boston Bar. The highway rose and fell along the contours of the canyon walls. I became intensely aware of my surroundings and the heat of the late afternoon. I was very thirsty and seemed to be constantly reaching down for a water bottle. The heat became more intense. I became intensely thirsty and drank all the water in my two flasks, and at one point, I heard my father's deep baritone voice saying, "Never let them say I raised a quitter." Head down, compelled by my father's admonition, I forced my unwilling legs to move, as I pushed on into the late afternoon, never giving up.

Around 7:30 p.m., I found a campground outside Boston Bar, where I ignored other campers and looked for an isolated spot as far away from them as possible. The campground regulations did not permit open fires, which meant that I could not heat the large can of soup I had transported up the canyon! And so, feeling exhausted and sorry for myself, I ate my cold soup, climbed into my sleeping bag and quickly fell asleep.

Day (3): 126 Km

July 10th
Total 381 Km

Boston Bar to Cache Creek

I woke early, snacked on nuts and fruit, and left the campground at 6:30 a.m. My first objective for the day was to climb Jackass Mountain, named for the poor old donkeys that fell into the Fraser Canyon during the 19th century "gold rush," when men and animals, loaded down with picks and shovels, travelled this road on their way to the goldfields of Northern British Columbia.

Jackass Mountain

The road was very steep, with the mountainside on my right and a loose gravel bank on the left that pitched down into the valley far below. The bike kept skidding and sliding through the loose gravel fallen onto the road from the mountain that loomed over me. The gradient became steeper, the bike path narrower, the climb more arduous, and I was forced to stand upright, pressing down on the pedals. I became concerned that they would snap with the pressure I was exerting.

Semi-trailers passed close to my arm, and I felt afraid that I might slip and fall beneath the wheels. I did not want to give in to the mountain but the idea of my journey ending beneath the monster wheels of a truck was sufficient to bring me to my senses. And so, I dismounted and crossed over to the gravel-free wide shoulder on the other side of the road, and from there, I pushed the bike and gear to the top.

On my way up the mountain, I found $1.25 in loose change and saw this as being a good omen, but I wondered how the coins had gotten there. I could see that there was no room for a vehicle to stop without creating a safety hazard, and I could not imagine people scattering coins out of the window as they drove by. Mumbling to myself, as I trudged up the hill, I concluded that the cycling gods had left the coins to encourage me on my journey!

At the top of Jackass Mountain, I stopped to look back into the canyon and across the valley to the misty blue mountain range on the far side. It was a rare moment of contemplation before the urge to keep moving, always moving forward, forced me back into the saddle once more.

Top of the mountain.

Heading for the junction with the Thompson River, the road began to snake up the side of the canyon wall and then down again. The downhills were exciting, but the climbs became very demanding. I finally stopped to wash and eat at a service station restaurant in Kanaka. But, the heat and stress of the climbs had reduced my otherwise immense appetite, and I could only munch on a small sandwich and a bowl of soup before moving on.

Gradually, the steep climbs and dips gave way to a wide valley floor and a smooth, even road that took me into Lytton, situated at the junction of the Fraser River and the Thompson River. I stopped the bike and looked back. I had survived the challenge of the Fraser Canyon, but I knew that there were more to come on this long journey to the east!

The Thompson High Desert

After Lytton, I took the Thompson River Valley Road, heading toward Cache Creek. The temperature exceeded 100 degrees Fahrenheit in the shade. I saw a shimmering heat haze floating over speckled hills and a dry yellow desert. Breathing in stifling hot air, sweat dripping down my face and into my eyes, losing sense of time and self, I entered an altered state of consciousness, floating outside myself in some kind of hypnotic trance: I was aware of cars filled with people, laughing, talking, sharing time together, as they passed by me, but no one shared my reality. I was alone on this highway, lost in time and space.

I cried in the heat between Spencer's Bridge and Cache Creek. My face was burning. I was exhausted and wanted only to escape this experience, but there was no release, no one to rescue me, and I could only push on and on through the pain and the heat. There was no turning back because there was nothing behind, only forward, always forward.

Head down, hands hard gripped to handlebars, seeing dead birds lying by the roadside: I witnessed their passing and blessed them as I went by. And then the road levelled out, the sounds faded, and I knew that I had overcome one more challenge on the long journey to be reunited with my children.

By late afternoon, I reached Brookside Campground outside Cache Creek, where I was able to set up my tent in a secluded area, build a fire, and consume a large can of Campbell's meat and vegetable soup, followed by two apples, a banana, and a bag of pastries I had purchased from a service station outside the campground. Obviously, my appetite had returned, but I was not feeling sociable and, once more, I kept myself isolated from other campers and thought only of this journey and the road ahead.

Day (4): 84 Km

July 11th
Total 460 Km

Cache Creek to Kamloops

I woke early, but it was a struggle to exchange my nice, comfortable sleeping bag for the harsh daily grind of the highway. I showered, shaved, packed up the tent, and made my way out of the campground. By 8:00 a.m., I had covered more than 30 kilometres of easy riding under a clear blue sky and perfect weather conditions. I was starting to feel tired and hungry, when I spotted a service station restaurant on the other side of the highway and decided to stop for breakfast.

I carefully parked and locked up the bike before entering the restaurant. Once inside, I was immediately overwhelmed by the noise. I saw groups of people sitting around small white tables scattered around the room. A blue haze from cigarette smoke filled the air. The clamour of competing conversations and the shrill cries of unattended children assaulted my hearing. I stood alone in the doorway, dressed in Velcro cycling shorts, knobbly knees, and a shiny sunburned face, deciding my next move.

Ignored by rotund servers bustling past with plates of hot food, I felt alienated from these people and my surroundings and wanted to leave this place, but my stomach refused to obey. Eventually, I was seated at small corner table, partially concealed from the other customers by a wooden partition, where I ordered a breakfast of french-fries, double bacon, eggs, coffee, and extra toast.

I felt exposed and threatened by all these noisy people in such an enclosed space. After the intense and silent experience of riding alone through the heat of the desert, I did not want to become involved or connected with any of them. I was afraid that if I let them come close, or become connected to me, I would be drawn into their "normal" world and lose the determination and resolve that had carried me to this point on my journey.

Breakfast consumed and no longer feeling hungry, I left the crowded restaurant and returned to the lonely isolation of the road. The temperature, once more climbed over 100 degrees Fahrenheit, and the ordeal that I had encountered yesterday returned. Cycling forward, focused on the rhythm and movement of my legs, spinning along, weightless and suspended in the heat, I entered the state of altered consciousness that I had experienced yesterday. I seemed to become one with the bike: unaware of cycling, unaware of thinking, simply moving forward in a dance with the road, endlessly unfolding before me.

After an hour of steady riding with only few cars or trucks going by, I saw two people standing on the crest of a hill beside a stationary vehicle. As I got closer, I could see that one of them, a woman, was holding something in her hand. They were a Dutch couple who had found the towel that I had left behind at the Cache Creek campground. They had passed me on the road and then waited patiently for my slow but steady arrival. I did not know them. I have no memory of seeing them at the campground, but they had seen me. I was moved by the kindness of these people, who had gone out of their way to assist a stranger on a bike, and I thanked them profusely. They smiled gently and, in broken English, wished me well on my journey before driving away. After they disappeared into the distance, I stood by the side of the-road, knowing that I was still on my own but no longer feeling so alone and alienated from others.

The day passed slowly, and I stopped briefly for a lunch of sandwiches and fruit that I ate by the side of the road, before cycling onward, dancing to the rhythm of the wheels, the hum of the tires, and the music of The Rolling Stones in my ears. The highway was empty and quiet. I noticed how convenient it was that the shoulder of the road had a nice white line to help me from straying into traffic. Then suddenly, I realized that I was riding on the divider line in the middle of the highway! Quickly pulling back to the bike path, I made a mental note to keep awake or at least stop drifting into a trance when sharing the road with passing traffic, especially big trucks.

On the outskirts of Kamloops, the back wheel began to vibrate. I stopped and discovered that the spokes of the wheel were bent out of shape, which meant that I had to make a detour of 10 kilometres into town to find a repair shop. I stopped a cyclist on the road, who provided directions to "Brown's Cycles." This was the name of the cycle shop in my hometown in England, which brought back memories of my life there so many years ago. He also advised me, in a thick Yorkshire accent, to watch out for the motorists in the town, who, according to him, did not seem to know the difference between a cyclist and a bump in the road, and were likely to run over both.

Mr. Brown of Brown's Cycles informed me that the heavy load over the rear wheel had bent the spokes out of shape. I could either buy a new wheel or have the spokes repaired, which he thought would merely provide a temporary solution to the problem. However, the cost of a new wheel would have significantly depleted my cash reserves and so I told him to just repair the spokes. Despite choosing the cheaper option, I still had difficulty handing over $8 to just repair the spokes and reset the brakes. However, I had carefully observed Mr. Brown, as he tightened the spokes and adjusted the brakes, thereby gaining valuable bike riding knowledge, that I felt sure would prove helpful in the days and weeks to come.

Riding out of town, and leaving Mr. Brown behind, I remembered how easy it had been when driving west with Jack, to drive off the highway for supplies and meals. But this time, instead of 20 minutes of air-conditioned comfort, I laboured for an hour each way before getting back to the highway.

Four kilometres past the junction into Kamloops, I came to a commercial campground located by the side of the highway. It was noisy and uninviting, filled with large camper vans squatting on concrete pads, but it was the only campground in the area, and I was exhausted from the heat. I set up my tent and shortly after met a young guy, his wife, and another couple with a huge camper van on the next campsite.

My little tent and bicycle, set up beside their huge camper van, must have looked strange and amusing to them. I wondered what they were going to make of my nightly ritual, when I started to scrounge around to find twigs and paper to light a fire and then proceed to boil a large can of Campbell's Vegetable Soup. However, I was saved from any possible social embarrassment by their kind invitation to join them under the shade of their canopy and share a meal of their far superior homemade stew.

They were kind and hospitable people, but I found it hard to relax and just chat with them. Once the meal was finished, I excused myself by claiming tiredness from cycling, and quickly returned to my campsite.

Late in the evening, I lay awake in the tent. I felt restless and unable to sleep. I was being drawn deeper and deeper into the most intense experience of my life. I was now fully committed to completing this long journey across my adopted land, but so much was happening. So many thoughts were passing through my mind that I could not record them all but only make scrambled notes in my small green journal for future reference.

Day (5): 114 Km

July 12th
Total 563 Km

Kamloops Campground to Salmon Arm

The campground road, leading to the highway, lay silent and empty in the early morning light. The people I had met last night were no longer part of my life. Only the road ahead and returning to my children were important to me now.

I thought again about the kindness of the young couple who had invited me to join them and share their lives as well as their food, but even when people were being kind and sociable, I had limited tolerance for their company and only wanted to retreat into the safe isolation of my self-determined world.

Later in the morning, I stopped by the roadside and talked with a couple who were cycling west from Michigan to Vancouver. Strong headwinds had forced them to give up on the Prairies and take the bus to continue their journey. I wanted to tell them about my experiences on the road, but I kept silent and maintained my distance. They seemed nice people, but I did not want to engage with them and make polite conversation. Once more, I had the opportunity to connect with others, but all I felt was the need to press on, going forward, separate and alone.

West of Chase

I cried as I climbed a steep, long hill west of Chase. During the climb, I felt an emotional pain, an old sorrow that I could not name. I cried aloud, but there was no one to hear, only the wind and the birds to witness my passing on this road into the mountains.

By noon, the temperature and humidity had increased. Coming into Chase, I decided to leave the highway and go for a swim in a small lake surrounded by tall green reeds. The water was cool and smooth to my skin, and I floated for a while in the centre of the lake gazing up at a clear blue sky. Suspended upon the surface of the lake, concealed from passing traffic, I stopped thinking and gave myself to the experience of this moment, a moment of relief from the intensity of the long journey. After my swim, I lay on a long flat rock by the side of the lake and fell asleep in the warm sun, until I was suddenly woken by the blaring sound of airbrakes from a passing truck, demanding that I wake up, move on and resume my journey.

Later in the afternoon, I found a small fishing rod lying by the side of the road and decided to take it with me. I had seen small streams and lakes beside the highway and in the campgrounds, and wondered if they contained fish. And so, with plans to add tasty fish to my evening diet of Campbell's Vegetable Soup, I purchased a fishing line and hooks at the next roadside service centre.

The sun continued to glare into my face, and despite a heavy layer of sunscreen, I was becoming burned, especially around the mouth. I was concerned about skin cancer and decided to use white zinc ointment to ensure maximum protection and forget about my appearance. Marked with white warrior paint, slashed diagonally across my face, I continued to ride to the east, becoming drawn even deeper into my subjective experience and away from any social connection with others.

Shortly before 3:30 p.m. I stopped to pick up fruit from a roadside fruit stand, including bananas, apples, three peaches, and three nectarines. All of it disappeared as I cycled along and munched away. Half an hour later, I stopped at another roadside stand for a large cheeseburger. One hour after that, two sausage rolls, and two cheese buns were consumed. Supper was a giant pizza sub, a can of peaches, and five apple turnovers. I could not stop thinking about food!

Before leaving Vancouver, I discovered that the normal daily calorie intake for an active adult male was around 2,500 calories. I knew that I would obviously need to consume more food than normal to obtain the energy required to cycle 9 hours or more every day. But the actual amount consumed was astonishing, and yet I always felt hungry. I would see a hill in the distance and immediately begin to feel hungry and think about food. And if Pavlov, the noted Russian psychologist, had been around to ring his bell when those hills appeared, like his experimental subjects, I might have drooled at the sound!

Coming into Chase, I noticed a change in the roadside vegetation. The undergrowth and trees along the highway became thicker, and I could smell the scent of pine trees drifting down from the high country to the east. I imagined filling my lungs with this clean mountain air when I faced the challenge of the steep climbs that lay ahead and felt encouraged by the image.

Late in the afternoon, as the temperature began to drop, I started to "flow" with the bike. Keeping an eye out for advancing traffic, standing upright on the pedals, I weaved along the road, dancing to the Motown Sound of Diana Ross and the Supremes. A butterfly played with me going up a long, slow hill, weaving and dancing, pulled along by my slipstream and then gliding away. And I became that butterfly, fragile in comparison to the roaring trucks coming up behind me. The truckers moved over to the middle of the road as they went by. I felt the pull of their slipstream, and I was drawn toward them, before falling back to regain the silent pathway that had now become my domain.

I reached the Green Tree Campground outside Salmon Arm around 6:00 p.m. The campground was quiet and empty. I set up my campsite, spoke to no one, cooked and ate my supper, and then crawled into the tent to retire for the night.

Day (6): 38 Km

July 13th
Total 600 Km

Salmon Arm to Cedars Campground

8:00 a.m., and I crawled slowly out of my sleeping bag, feeling tired and rundown. Showered, packed up my gear, and returned to the road before 9:00 a.m. After 15 minutes of cycling, I began to feel listless, tired, and bored with my life on the road, so I decided to stop for a rest day at the first decent looking campground that I came to on the highway.

I remember riding and laughing aloud going up the hill from Salmon Arm. A choir of birds concealed in the bushes beside the road, sang in harmony as I passed by. Steadily, I cycled east toward the mountains, silently chanting, calming my mind, opening to the experience of the journey, living in the moment, being here, now.

On a hill outside Sicamous, I stopped the bike and stood beside a plaque overlooking the lake below. The plaque described the history of the area, noting that the lake takes its name from the Shuswap, the northernmost band of the Salishan Nation of British Columbia. I stood silently reading about this Indigenous group of more than 5,000 people who had roamed freely for centuries over a vast land of lakes and forests, stretching over 150 miles to the west, north, and east.

Lake of The Shuswap

And as I stood there, gazing over the lake below, I lost my sense of time and place and experienced a strange and powerful awareness that I had lived a past life as one of those ancient people, who had lived in this beautiful place. The vision ended, and it felt as though I had been asleep or dreaming, standing beside my bike on that high point. Eventually, I climbed back onto the bike and drifted along the road, feeling calm and at peace, feeling connected to the land and the life around me.

I decided to stop for an exceptionally large late breakfast outside Sicamous before slowly cycling on to Cedars Campground, arriving there just after noon. After setting up my tent, I slept the rest of the afternoon and then tried my luck, fishing in a small stream using a worm as bait. Unfortunately, and with disappointment, I failed to catch anything. I made a note to try a piece of ham or something more appealing than the local worms the next time.

After first heating and then eating my supper, I wandered around the campground and met the Cole family, consisting of Margaret, Roger, and their teenage son, Richard. Because I had taken it easy and rested for a good part of the day, I was feeling more sociable and interested in their company. We talked about the trip, and they seemed very curious, especially why I was doing it! I was not sure that my explanation made any sense to them, but I felt relaxed and at ease as we talked and shared biking stories.

And, later, as the sun was setting and the forests became still and silent, I sat outside my tent, thinking about this day, and the vision I had experienced, as I gazed down upon the beautiful Lake of The Shuswap, and I felt grateful for my life and being in this place.

Day (7): 65 Km

July 14th
Total 665 Km

Cedars Campsite to Revelstoke

I left the campground shortly before 8:00 a.m. Initially, I felt relaxed and comfortable and was looking forward to the ride and my day on the road. However, as the temperature increased, my energy began to fade. I cycled along feeling detached, bored, and irritable. I could hear a critical voice, muttering in the background of my mind, telling me that I had spent too much time chatting with the Cole family, instead of sleeping and preparing for today.

Thirty kilometres and over two hours later, I had still not found a restaurant to have breakfast. I was hungry and irritated, pushing hard and standing upright on the pedals, as I climbed a steep hill outside Three Valley Gap, when the back tire suddenly started to wobble. I stopped and examined the wheel, which seemed bent and twisted out of alignment. I could see that my bike repair skills could not solve this problem, which meant I had to find a way to get to Revelstoke, 25 kilometres down the road, where I might find a bicycle repair shop.

I removed the offending wheel and stood beside the road, holding the wheel by my side, where it could be seen, and sticking out my hand, thumb pointing upward in the prescribed manner, hoping for a ride into town. During the next twenty minutes, five or six cars went by without stopping. I must have appeared alien and strange to these ordinary travellers of the highway, with shiny white zinc ointment slashed across my cheekbones and a dismantled bicycle at my feet;

all of which may have contributed to their lack of interest in my predicament!

Eventually, I got a ride from Gordon and Ray, who were driving a large van that was big enough to accommodate my bike, bags, and me. Gordon had a small business in Calgary, where he sold promotional items for sporting events, and was returning with his brother, Ray, from a golf tournament in Kamloops.

Fifteen minutes later, we arrived in Revelstoke, where I discovered that the bike shop did not open until the next day! Gordon kindly waited for me while I shopped for food supplies and then gave me a ride back to a commercial campground on the outskirts of town that had hot showers, laundromat, and good sites spread out from each other. I found an excellent campsite, located away from the crowded areas, and set up my tent.

Nestled in under small trees and concealed from curious eyes, ensconced once more in my own little world, I rested during the afternoon, and then caught up on laundry, had a shower, collected twigs for the evening campfire, and made notes in my journal. I planned to get up early in the morning and head into town to get the tire repaired. By leaving the bike at the campground, all packed and ready to go, I could then head for Rogers Pass without delay. I hoped that with this plan, and if all went well with the tire repair, tomorrow would be the day that I would face the daunting challenge of climbing to the top of the high mountain pass.

Revelstoke Campsite

Having rested and with a clear plan of action for tomorrow, I cautiously ventured out of my secluded campsite and started talking to other campers. I heard that forest fires were burning around Golden, 80 kilometres east of Rogers Pass. One camper told me that he had seen three fires along the highway between Golden and Rogers Pass, which was not encouraging news. Later, I spoke to a couple biking from Lake Louise in Alberta to Vancouver, who told me that they had considered taking The Fraser Canyon route but thought that the canyon and its tunnels were too dangerous. I agreed with them but did not go into details concerning my "encounter" with the tunnels in case they decided that I was certifiable!

I felt encouraged by my newfound sociability, but the need to consume calories asserted its authority and eventually I wandered back to my own campsite, prepared my evening meal, and reflected on the day.

The delay in the repair had forced me to revise my estimates and plans, but these changes were becoming easier to manage. I had left Vancouver on that first day with my thoughts and attention totally focussed on gaining distance and making progress toward my destination. I had to return to Vancouver for the tent and equipment that I had forgotten and felt pursued by the fear of failure caused by this unexpected problem. But now I am adapting to my life on the road. I am still faced with unexpected events that cancel or frustrate my plans and schedules, but I am responding in a more flexible and adaptive manner.

Day (8) 125 Km

July 15th
Total 790 Km

Revelstoke to Marl Creek Campground

I woke early, quickly showered, packed up the tent and gear in preparation for leaving the campground, and then sat around for half an hour waiting for Ray, a nice guy I had met in the laundry room last night, who had kindly offered to drive me into town to pick up the repaired wheel. Arriving at the bike shop, I described my problem to the technician and explained that I was on my way to Toronto and was falling behind schedule. He was sympathetic to my predicament and promised to give my repair top priority. I could pick up the wheel in about an hour, which gave me the opportunity to head into the restaurant next door for breakfast.

Once the wheel had been straightened and the spokes adjusted, I hitch-hiked back to the campground. I said goodbye to the people I had encountered around the campground the previous night, and was back on the road, heading for Roger's Pass before 11 a.m. The warm and sunny weather was ideal for cycling and I drifted along the road without a care in the world, feeling particularly good about life and myself. After an hour of steady cycling, I stopped to obtain ice-fresh water from a stream by the side of the road, where I sat quietly for 10 minutes, just listening to the music of the stream, the sounds of the forest and experiencing a sense of contentment and connection in this peaceful place.

46 kilometres past of Revelstoke, I came to the first of the snow sheds I would encounter on the road to Roger's Pass. These snow

sheds had been constructed over the highway to deflect the massive snow avalanches that crash down from the mountains during the winter months. Even though they were shorter, wider and had better ventilation than the Fraser Canyon tunnels, I knew that I had to treat them with respect and recognize the risks that they posed for any cyclist venturing into them.

Before entering Lanark snow shed, the first and the longest of the six sheds, I stopped the bike and reached into the front pannier to exchange my sunglasses for my clear lens prescription glasses and discovered that I had left them behind at the campground! I thought of cycling back to the campground to retrieve them, but then I remembered the long and lonely ride through the morning traffic back into Vancouver on the first day. And, in that moment, I knew with absolute certainty that I could not turn round and cycle back in the wrong direction again.

I sat by the roadside, not knowing what to do, my mind churning, as I searched for solutions to this crisis. And then I remembered sitting by the stream earlier in the day, feeling calm and connected to the life around me and my mind began to clear. After moments of quiet breathing, I decided to accept my loss and continue without my glasses. I still had a pair of prescription sunglasses and decided that they would be good enough for me to see in the snow shed and on the road during the day. It did not occur to me that this strategy would inevitably fail if I had to ride at night in the dark for any reason!

Having made my decision, I got back on the bike and entered the Lanark snow shed. The bike pathway was wider and easier to ride than the Fraser tunnels, and I now felt physically stronger and more confident about my riding ability. Peering over the top of my sunglasses, I dodged the debris and litter on the path, sprinting for the light at the end of a long straight bike path. I heard my bellowing voice echoing through the tunnel, roaring at any trucks that came close; not that anyone heard or cared, but I found it helpful!

I have no clear memories or recollection of the road after the Lanark snow shed. I was now making the run to Roger's Pass and my mind became focused with a singular intensity on the task that lay before me. I can only recall that gradually, the road began to rise into the sky, climbing higher and higher. I was already feeling tired and knew that it would be a long time before I got the benefit of a downhill run, but I knew that there was no turning back or stopping to rest. I was now fully committed. I ignored my fatigue and continued to climb steadily.

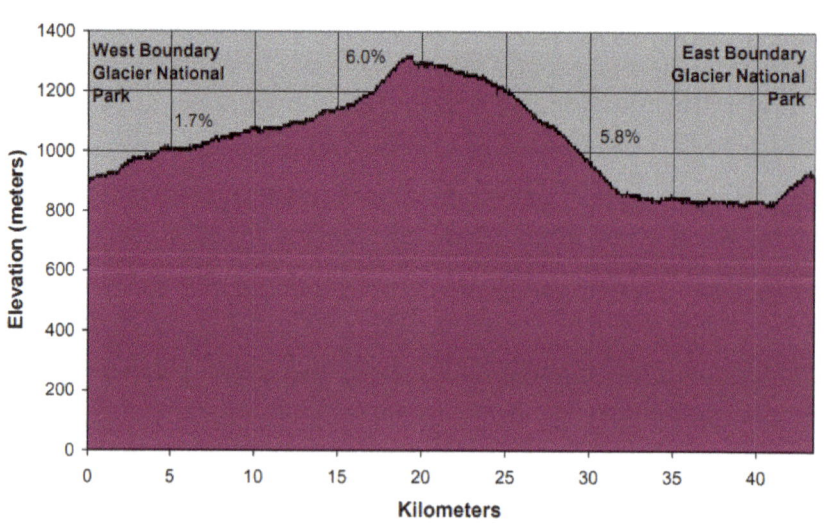

---

[1] **Stat Credits: Govt. of British Columbia**

There were moments of pain in the silence of that empty road when I roared and shouted with anger to get to the top of a steep incline. I refused to give in and get off the bike. I remembered my school days when I played rugby football; roaring like a mad bull, carrying players on my back or pulling on my legs, as they tried to stop me from scoring. I remember thinking, then and now, I was not going to be defeated: I was going to the top of Roger's Pass, and nothing was going to stop me! And then the road levelled out and I entered the first of the smaller Glacier Park snow sheds. I quickly cycled through the four remaining sheds and knew that I only had one very steep climb before arriving at Rogers Pass!

The Rocky Mountains

My heart was pumping fast as I slowly cycled into the parking lot at the top of the pass and stopped the bike. I felt subdued by the silence of this place, mysterious and sacred in the strange light that filtered through the scattered pine trees. I sat on the bike for 5 minutes, feeling a winter chill in the summer air, absorbing the sensations of the place and the significance of this moment. This was the point on my journey, when I could finally say that I had climbed over The Rocky Mountains on a bike, and I had done it without having to dismount! I remember thinking that, regardless of what might happen in the future, this moment would always stand out as a peak experience in my life!

I could see tourists standing in small groups around the bus coaches that had brought them here. Eventually, I placed my bike and gear beside a wall where I could keep an eye on them and slowly walked over to these people. I stood beside them, listening to their conversations. People approached me, asking questions. They wanted to know where I had come from and what my destination was. They were obviously intrigued by my presence and appearance in this isolated spot, and their attention left me feeling like some kind of celebrity, a person of importance no less.

Leaving the tourists chattering and laughing beside their tour coaches, I went into a large gift store, where I purchased food supplies and postcards. I spoke to a young woman in her late teens who told me that she was planning to ride to Vancouver from Calgary in the fall. She told me that she had been cycling 80-90 kilometres a day in preparation for her ride. I neglected to tell her of the "get fit on the road strategy" that I had used in preparation for my own trip. I met a gentleman in his mid-sixties, with a rich Scottish accent and warm brown eyes, who came up to me in the store. He talked about his experiences as a young man, cycling in the highlands of Scotland, and told me he was travelling across Canada by train and bus to fulfill a lifetime dream.

I kept talking non-stop with anyone who approached me. I could still feel the energy that had carried me to the top of this mountain pass. I wanted to shout and roar to express what I had just achieved, but I kept quiet and enjoyed my moment of fame!

After an hour at the top of the mountain pass, I left the people and the chatter behind and settled into the rhythm of the bike and the road ahead. Heading downhill, gradually gathering speed, I gave the bike permission to fly. The road was clear and falling away with no traffic in sight and a wide bike path. I moved my hands to the centre of the handlebars, lowered my head, and let the bike run faster and faster. Suddenly I realized that it would be dangerous if I attempted to brake and, with that thought in mind, I focused my attention on this moment, this split second, as I hurtled down the mountainside. The weight of the bike, the heavy gear, and my willingness to let it happen, all contributed to the accelerating speed.

I became intensely aware of the gravel on the shoulder of the road. I could see each tiny pebble, each twig, each indentation in my path, and with a quick flick of my wrist and hands, I avoided them. No thoughts anymore, just a total focus on the narrow path, my vision narrowed and razor-sharp. Going faster now; too late to stop. A sudden thought that I could crash and smash into the ground, ending my life. I forced the thought and the image out of awareness. I was aware of the risk, but I ignored the danger and gave myself to the experience. I was flying! It was exhilarating!

I do not know how long this intense mad ride lasted, but slowly and gently, I applied the brakes, bringing the bike to a halt. My breath slowed, my mind cleared, sun warmed my face. I felt incredibly alive and awake! I sat by the side of the road for at least ten minutes. During that time, two or three cars went by, but I was absorbed in the "experience" of my wild ride down the mountainside and paid them no attention.

Despite a delayed start, the long, slow climb up to Rogers Pass, and my extended celebrity moment at the top, I was still able to make Marl Creek campground before 6:00 p.m., no doubt helped by the 60 kilometres downhill 'thunderbolt' run from Rogers Pass.

Supper consisted of a full packet of macaroni and cheese combined with Kellogg's raisin bran flakes, making a very filling supper; enough for six people! And, as the mountain light faded into darkness, feeling exhausted, grubby, and very satisfied with myself, I climbed into my sleeping bag and quickly fell asleep.

Day (9): 85 Km

July 16th
Total 875 Km

Marl Creek Campground to Hoodoo Creek Campground

I managed to scramble out of my sleeping bag and onto the road before 6:00 a.m. It was very cold in the early morning at this high altitude, but fortunately, I had warm cycling gloves to protect my hands and a fine woollen hat to keep my head warm. I wanted to reach Golden before 10:00 a.m., hoping to find a restaurant for breakfast, but the hills were difficult to climb, and my progress was slow. Halfway up a very steep hill, I stood upright on the pedals, pushing down hard, forcing the bike to climb the steep gradient, when suddenly the back wheel started to wobble, and I nearly fell over. I stopped the bike and pulled over to the side of the road, removed the wheel, tightened up the spokes, and was back on the road again in less than fifteen minutes. I remember feeling quite pleased and proud of modest bike repair skills.

On a level stretch of road, just before Golden, I met two young guys, Jeff and Gill, riding light bikes, and staying in motels. We stopped by the side of the road, exchanged pleasantries, and shared stories of the road and conditions we had encountered. I had a negative reaction to Gill, who wanted to dominate the conversation with his know-it-all advice! He was helpful but competitive, and I responded likewise.

I arrived in Golden shortly before 10:30 a.m. and consumed a huge breakfast at a roadside restaurant. Cycling out of town, I began to emit copious amounts of gas, which no doubt accelerated my forward momentum, but may also have disturbed the local wildlife. I made a note, for future reference, that my novel mix of macaroni, cheese, and raisin-bran flakes, that I had consumed for supper, did not blend too well with late-morning breakfasts of sausage, eggs and bacon!

And then the rain and thunder came from the east to greet me. The rain was light, but the thunder was impressive. Great booming sounds, like timpani drums being pounded by giants, echoing from mountain peak to mountain peak and down into the valleys below. I felt small and insignificant, overpowered by a force that I could not ignore. I stopped the bike and stood alone by the side of that high empty road, feeling very vulnerable, but strangely, connected to and accepted by this energy of the mountains that vibrated through my body and filled the space around me.

I was proud of my success in riding over Rogers Pass and felt confident that the much shorter climb over Kicking Horse Pass would not be a problem. But I did not want to push my luck and decided to stay overnight at Hoodoo Creek Campground and then make the assault on Kicking Horse Pass tomorrow when my energy would be stronger.

The campground was set back 500 metres from the highway, at the end of a long, heavily forested road. Once more, on my own in a campsite set back in the forest, and away from other campers, I sat outside the tent and wrote in my journal. And later, as dusk gave way to the night and the forest became quiet, I curled up in my sleeping bag and fell asleep, dreaming of easy downhill riding in the days to come.

Day (10): 110 Km

July 17th
Total 985 Km

Hoodoo Creek Campground to Banff Tunnel Mountain Campground

Drifting out of dreaming in the early morning light, I heard heavy rain on the tent roof. This did not sound very encouraging, so I turned over and went back to sleep! Snoozed on for another hour or so until the rain stopped, then got up, showered, packed, and was ready to depart by 7:30 a.m.

It was incredibly quiet, and no one was around as I slowly cycled out of the campground. Suddenly, I heard a loud grunting, coughing sound coming from a clearing 20-30 yards away from the path. I stopped the bike and walked over to the clearing, where I discovered a medium-sized brown bear inside a cage on wheels. I slowly moved closer, making what I imagined to be soft encouraging bear-like noises, until I was five feet from the cage when the bear suddenly went for me. I cannot recall ever seeing anything move that fast as it lashed out against the side of the cage. I was amazed at the speed of its strike, which seemed faster than a cat! I found out later that the Park Wardens trap any bears who find their way from the forest into the campground looking for food. Quite convenient, I thought, to have your bear trapped and ready to go, prepackaged in a cage with wheels!

Bear in a Cage

I had intended to eat breakfast at Field, and then make the climb to Kicking Horse Pass. However, when I arrived at Field at 9:00 a.m., I discovered that the restaurant was closed, which left me with no choice except to continue climbing upward to the pass, hoping to find somewhere to eat on the way up.

The climb was long and difficult. Just before 11 a.m., I reached the top of the pass, where I found a restaurant and had breakfast. The bill for my farmer's sausage, eggs, hash browns, and toast came to $8.40, which I justified as a reward for my efforts in getting to the top of the pass!

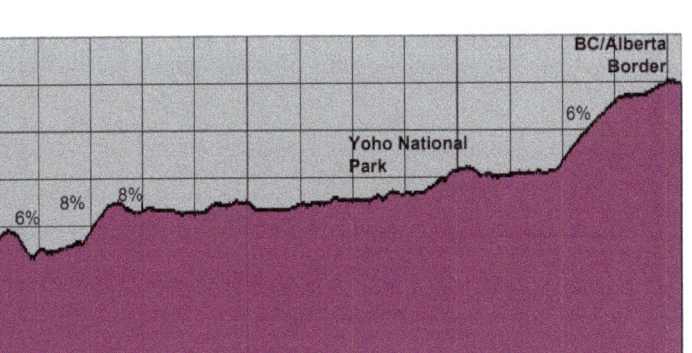

Hwy 1 - Kicking Horse Pass

After a gentle downhill ride of approximately 10 kilometres, I arrived at the junction leading into Lake Louise Village. From my journey west with Jack, I remembered the beauty of the lake and the snow-capped mountains that surrounded it and was tempted to leave the highway to experience it once more, but decided to push on to Banff, 60 kilometres east of the junction.

The ride down to Banff was quick and easy, but three kilometres outside the town, the spokes on the back tire started to rattle, and then the tire itself collapsed. I sat down beside the road and removed the wheel. Repaired the tire's inner tube and tried to tighten the spokes again, only to discover that the metal rim of the tire was bent out of shape and beyond my repair skills. I sat by the roadside, intent on the repair job when a pick-up truck stopped beside me. "Need any help, dude?" a voice cried out of the van window. And that was how I met

---

[2] **Stat Credits: Govt. of British Columbia**

two guys who worked at a bike shop in Banff called "The Park and Peddle." They gave me a ride to the bike shop, where I described the problem with the tire rim and the chronic difficulties I had been having with it. The senior bike technician advised me that my wheels, especially the back wheel, were not designed to carry the combined weight of the camping gear and myself. I was told that if I wanted to avoid the problems that I had been having, I had to purchase a custom-made, heavy-duty bike wheel. However, the wheel had to be constructed in the shop and would not be ready until tomorrow.

I borrowed a used wheel from the repair shop, attached it to the bike, and headed in the direction of the Banff campground, located on a hill leading out of town. I remember feeling very discouraged as I rode through the downtown area of Banff on a bike with no gears, and a squeaky front wheel. In addition, the new wheel was going to cost $56 plus tax, which seemed an incredible amount since the entire bike had only cost $110. Once more, I felt dismayed at the unexpected costs that were showing up like uninvited rats, to gnaw away at my dwindling cash reserves.

I set up camp, and then, like a lost and hungry bear, I left the bike locked to a campsite wooden table and wandered back into town looking for food. There was no shortage of restaurants and fast-food outlets in this tourist town, but I was concerned about the cost of the new wheel and decided to forgo the luxury of a restaurant meal and pick up food supplies to make supper back at the campground.

Feeling hungry, I wandered through a huge Safeway supermarket in a daze, looking at mounds of food but unable to choose anything. Eventually, I purchased a collection of miscellaneous items, including my staple diet of canned soup, and walked back to the campground, where I cooked my evening meal, listened to music on my CD player, and then drifted off to sleep as the light began to fade.

Day (11): 40 Km

July 18th
Total 1025 Km

Banff to Bow Valley Provincial Park

Woke up around 7:30 a.m. and had a leisurely shower. I then packed up the tent and gear in preparation for my eventual departure and left them at the campground office.

Sitting astride my bike, complete with squeaking wheel broadcasting my progress, like some kind of ice-cream truck advertising its wares, I free- wheeled downhill from the campground into town, where I quickly made my way to the busy cycle shop located on the main street.

I was anxious to have the new wheel and be riding out of town as soon as possible, but my eager enthusiasm for an early start was replaced by disappointment, when I was informed that it was going to be at least two hours before the wheel would be ready. I considered my limited options, and then shrugged off the disappointment, and left the shop in search of a restaurant where I could get breakfast. Fortunately, there was a restaurant next door to the bike shop, with a budget breakfast menu in the widow. I found a table with a window view of the street and took my time with a leisurely breakfast and caught up with my daily journal notes. After breakfast, I left the restaurant to pass time before the wheel was ready by taking a closer look at Banff.

The downtown area was filled with cyclists and small groups of people dressed in snazzy fashionable outfits, and I wanted to be part of this happy carefree throng of holiday makers. Conscious of previously wanting to be separate and on my own, it felt strange that I now wanted to connect with the people I encountered. After breakfast, I ambled around the immediate vicinity of the bike shop, just trying to blend in, looking into shop windows and pretending to be just another tourist, waiting for the chance to start a conversation or to make contact. But no one looked at me or spoke to me.

I had become invisible and did not belong. I was not one of them and I felt alienated by the experience. The mountain looming at the end of the main street was overpowering; a gigantic presence glaring down, telling me that I was not wanted in this place and that I should leave.

With a brand-new heavy-duty wheel attached to the bike, and the gears working smoothly, I climbed the hill back to the campground, where I picked up my gear and set off for The Bow Valley. I had expected a fast comfortable, downhill 35-kilometre ride to the Bow Valley campground. However, I had to deal with small but demanding hills that slowed my progress, and I lost more time by having to make a 10-kilometre round trip into Canmore to purchase food supplies.

I reached the Bow Valley campground in the late afternoon and found a secluded campsite by the side of The Bow River. I was immediately captivated by the beauty of the surroundings. The Bow Valley was magnificent. I felt the presence of the river, the mountains and became absorbed by the scene. I sat outside my tent and watched the sun going down through the trees, creating shadows and pathways of light to mark the passing day. I looked at the gentle light, reflected on the moving highway of the river, and felt a sorrow and regret that had no name, a familiar feeling, a hidden loneliness that seemed to have been with me most of my life: constantly leaving the familiar places and the people who loved me and finding myself alone in the world; constantly embarking upon adventures like this journey; constantly discovering myself in loneliness; always questioning and searching for answers.

Later, in the tent, after I had cooked and eaten supper, I remembered an experience, a moment in time when I first experienced the pain of separation, of being alone:

The Bow Valley

I was three years of age, and England was at war. My father had enlisted in the armed forces and was absent from the home. I was often alone in the house with a teenage girl named Joyce, whom my mother had brought into the home to help with the housework and care for me when she was away.

One day, my mother returned from her work. I remember standing in the kitchen, watching as she removed her dark blue raincoat and the broad black hat with the silver crest in the centre, which identified her as the 'District Midwife.' I could see that she was tired. I heard the sharp, angry sound of her voice asking a question, and I heard Joyce reply, "It was Thomas who did it, not me."

I looked at my mother's face and saw the hurt and sadness. And then I heard Joyce say, "He broke it when I wasn't looking." I did not know what she was saying but I heard my name, and I knew there was something wrong. And when I saw the effect of her words upon my mother's face, I knew that she was lying. I waited for my mother to say something, to tell Joyce that she did not believe her, but she remained silent, and I could only see tiredness and a sad disappointment in her face.

Suddenly, I felt anxious, angry, and confused. I felt a tight, hard tension in my arms and a contraction of my hands into hard little balls pressed hard against my body. I saw my mother's eyes gaze reproachfully at me, and I felt afraid and hurt because she did not know what was in my heart.

And in that moment, I became self-conscious and aware of being alone and emotionally separated from her. I remember the anger, hurt, and sense of injustice that I felt when I turned to look directly at Joyce, point my finger at her, and say: "I did not do it. Joyce did it." I saw the quick look, the attempt to hold my eyes, and then her gaze shifted, and she looked away, unable to deny the accusation and the truth in my voice. I heard the change of tone in my mother's voice. I could hear anger as she spoke to Joyce. I do not remember what she said, but I knew that she believed me. I felt restored to her and waited for her to turn and hold me. But she turned away to walk into the living room, and I stood alone once more feeling confused and hurt. I did not understand what had happened, but I knew that something had changed and would never be the same again."

Lying awake in the tent, remembering childhood memories of being alone, of feeling separate and having to find my own way, I felt discouraged that I would have to face at least three weeks of being alone on the highway, peddling the bike day after day across the vast empty Prairies. I knew that I could not maintain the focus and sheer determination that had enabled me to cope with the Fraser Canyon and climb over the Rockies. I knew that I had to find a different strategy to cope with the challenge of cycling across the Prairies.

Soothed by the calming sound of The Bow River, flowing past my campsite, letting go of thinking and planning for the days to come, I fell asleep.

Day (12): Rest Day

July 19th
Total 1025 Km

Bow Valley Provincial Park

During the night I woke up, feeling slightly nauseous and anxious. In the morning, I had a headache and still felt nauseous and tired. I had brought a thermometer with me, as part of my small emergency medical kit, and so I took my temperature, thinking I might have a fever, but the results were normal. I wondered if I was experiencing the delayed effect of climbing over the mountains. And so, I decided to fast and rest to give my body a chance to recuperate. The day was spent in the tent drifting in and out of sleep and feeling mildly depressed.

Late afternoon, lying on the sleeping bag inside the tent, I struggled with competing notions. On the one hand, I did not want to cycle the 12-kilometre round trip into Seebe to purchase supplies, but I had nothing to eat all day, and I was hungry. Eventually, I stopped ruminating, scrambled off the sleeping bag, and set off to find food.

Returning from the convenience store in Seebe, food supplies purchased, I felt energized and optimistic once more. The late afternoon sunlight was warm and clear, and the tree-lined road leading to the campground was flat and straight. I could see a bunch of riders ahead, and as I approached them, I began to move up through the gears, smoothly and easily picking up speed. Instead of the extra weight of the tent and equipment, I carried just one carrier bag containing food for the evening meal; I felt weightless and could fly. I heard shouting as I swept by them, and a voice cried out, saying, "I want to ride like that." Looking back into the rear-view mirror, I saw a couple of the riders had broken away from the group and were coming after me, so I switched gears, picked up speed, and left them far behind!

After cooking and eating my usual evening meal, I sat outside the tent and watched the evening light slowly fade over the snow-capped Rocky Mountains I looked over the waters of the river, at those mountains, knowing that I had climbed over them on my old bike without getting off once, and no one could take that achievement from me.

Day (13): 215 Km

July 20th
Total 1240 Km

Bow Valley Provincial Park to Bassano

1400 Kilometres of Flat Prairie Road

I woke early and was able to leave the campground shortly before 6:15 a.m. I was hungry, but it took a good 40 kilometres of hard riding before I found a roadside restaurant for breakfast. And then, it took another 40 kilometres of cycling through the heavy commuter and commercial traffic flowing in and out of Calgary, before I returned to the open highway again.

I had left the city behind and was about to enter the next stage of my journey. I stopped the bike and looked at an endless flat open road disappearing into the vast emptiness of the open Prairies, and I knew that I was looking at my future laid out before me.

As I rode across that flat prairie highway, I found it difficult to gauge the distance from one point to another. The presence of poplar trees on the far horizon, first perceived as a faint smudge in the shimmering heat of the road, stood silently awaiting my arrival. Holding the image of that distant marker in my mind, I bent my head down, and started to count my breath, breathing in and breathing out in a steady focused rhythm. I remember listening to the haunting music of panpipes on my cd player, the humming tires and the clicking sound of pedals as I cycled toward the distant horizon. After a while, I lifted my head and saw the trees coming closer. The next time I looked, the trees had disappeared, only to reappear as another faint smudge, standing silently on another distant horizon. There are more poplar trees on the Prairies than most highway travellers would imagine unless, of course, they are riding a bicycle with time to notice these things!

Sometime around 3 p.m., I reached Strathmore, having covered approximately 130 kilometres safter leaving The Bow Valley campground. I stopped for a late lunch at a Husky service station on the highway. And there, I met up again with Gill and Jeff, who had been taking their time relaxing in their motel and enjoying the tourist delights of Banff and Calgary. We spent time talking and sharing stories of life on the road and the events that had occurred since our last meeting. We then said our goodbyes and returned to the highway, where, despite my heavier load, I was able to keep up with them for about two kilometres. And then, they moved into a high fast gear and left me behind. I watched them gradually becoming smaller and smaller, until they disappeared into the distance, leaving me alone on the road once more. I remember feeling slightly envious of their fast light bikes and comfortable motel rooms, but then I remembered the reasons for undertaking my journey and I cycled on.

The wind was at my back and, even though I was feeling hungry, I decided to snack on my emergency food supplies, push on toward Bassano, and camp at the first commercial campground on the highway.

Somewhere around 7:00 p.m. it dawned on me that there were no campgrounds between Strathmore and Bassano. I was anxious not to get stranded on the highway again when nightfall came, and so I pulled off the road and cycled up a long winding dirt road to a farmhouse to ask permission to camp. But there was no one home. I did not want to camp on private property without permission and risk an encounter with belligerent farm hands returning home in the middle of the night, so I returned to the highway and began to ride harder, head down, starting to feel anxious. Reflected in the little rear-view mirror mounted on the handlebar, I could see the sun going down behind me. And then the light and my vision began to fade. I was peering over the rims of my sunglasses, and hoping I did not hit a rock or branch on the road: I was racing against time and the setting sun!

Finally, just before nightfall, I reached Bassano and quickly found a municipal campground that possessed a primitive washroom but no showers. I was exhausted and just wanted to sleep. Motivated by gigantic prairie mosquitoes, feasting on every inch of my tender exposed flesh, I managed to set up the tent in record time. And so, with flailing arms and muttered curses, intended to intimidate any persistent mosquitoes that may have followed me into the tent, I clambered into my sleeping bag and fell into a deep and dreamless sleep.

Day (14): 60 Km

July 21ˢᵗ
Total 1300 Km

Bassano to Tillebrook Provincial Park

I slept until 8:00 a.m. Quickly showered, packed up my tent, and paid for my campsite on the way out. I had a large breakfast at a restaurant in Bassano and was back on the highway before 10:00 a.m. I felt physically strong and fit and surprised at how quickly I had recovered from the stress and fatigue of the previous day.

The east wind was a fierce pressure, blowing directly into my face, I was forced to lower my head. It was hard going in this strong and constant wind. I listened to the hypnotic humming of spinning tires and, lifting my head for a moment, saw a hawk flying low across the prairie fields, searching for gophers. I saw grasshoppers eating dead grasshoppers, strewn like confetti along the grey gravel path below me. I heard the mad cries of seagulls, shrieking like banshees as I passed by. And then the silence of the empty road returned once more, stretching endlessly into the distance.

The wind became stronger, blowing hard into my face. I stopped thinking and bowed my head in submission. And then, I left my body to float high above the prairie landscape. Flying free, I looked down and saw a tiny creature, an insect on wheels, moving slowly across a vast open plain.

The Prairies were different. After each uphill struggle in The Rockies, I experienced the reward of a downhill glide for my efforts. But the long, flat prairie road was relentless in its demand that I keep pushing against the pedals, endlessly pushing, hour after hour without reward.

I reached Brooks around 1:00 p.m. and stopped for lunch at a Shell service station restaurant on the highway. Half an hour later, I was back on the bike. Head bent low, cycling into that wind, I chanted the mantra that had carried me through the Fraser Canyon and the heat of the high desert country. Periodically, I would look up and, at one point, I saw a sign pointing to Tillebrook Provincial Campground, 6 kilometres further down the road. I was tempted to stop, get off the highway, out of the wind, and rest, but my motivation was strong, and I had far to go that day, so I bowed my head once more and cycled on.

Suddenly, between one breath and the next, the world ended, and I ceased to exist! Struck, crushed, dying, skull split open – I experienced a dreadful blackness without thought, a moment of intense fear, and then nothing- just a silent empty vacuum. I do not know how long I remained in that timeless place. And then, I was conscious again, lying on my back, gazing up at clouds in a clear blue sky. Slowly, my mind began to clear. I heard a solitary hawk crying in the wind, and I became aware of my surroundings.

I was lying beneath a large metal hopper attached to the back of a huge potash truck, parked on the hard shoulder of the road. I do not know how long I had been lying there. I could only cry out for help in a voice that seemed faint and far away, but no one responded. Then, I heard and saw a heavy truck coming toward me from behind. Unable to move, I lay outstretched on the ground and raised my hand for help. The truck slowed as it passed me, and I saw the face of the truck driver. He glanced down at me without expression as though I was an object, some kind of roadkill, before he revved the engine, increased speed, and drove away, leaving me alone once more, lying on the side of the road.

Eventually, I managed to stand and lean against the side of the truck. There was blood on my face, blood on my hands. I had a gash on my forehead, and I could feel an intense but dull, heavy pain in my neck where I had been injured eight months earlier. I checked the bike with a glance. It seemed fine, with no damage, which was strange, given the force of the impact that I had experienced. Then, I saw that the bike seat had been forced down to the crossbar. I realized that instead of crashing into the truck, the front wheel of the bike had slipped beneath the edge of the hopper, and my forehead had struck the metal rim, abruptly halting the forward motion of the bike. The force of the impact had then travelled down my spine to the bike seat.

After a minute or two, I heard the truck door being opened. A man climbed out of the cab and slowly walked up to me. He paused and said, "I had to stop to check a leaking radiator. Saw you coming up the hill." He then asked, "Are you all right?" and before I could reply, he turned away and began to inspect his truck for damage.

I leaned against the truck and looked at this driver in his dirty blue coveralls and saw that he was holding two bright orange safety cones in his hands. He slowly walked away from me and carefully placed them on the side of the road about 20 feet back from the truck. Once satisfied that the cones would warn any traffic coming up from behind, he turned round, walked past me in silence, and climbed back into his truck. I realized that he had forgotten to place safety cones on the road to warn traffic of his stationary vehicle and his only concern was to protect himself from legal liability.

I stood, leaning against the truck for about ten minutes, feeling confused and disoriented. I was unable to think clearly or decide what to do next. And then I remembered the sign I had seen earlier, pointing to the campground down the road. After straightening the seat, I carefully climbed back on the bike and slowly began to cycle toward the campground. I arrived there half an hour later, somewhere around midday.

Somehow, I managed to set up my tent, groundsheet, and sleeping bag. I climbed inside the tent, feeling confused, unable to think, and lay down. I remember the pain and stiffness in my neck and shoulders. I felt very tired and wanted to rest. But sleep would not come, just fast, anxious thoughts tumbling through my mind. And then, slowly, consciousness slipped away, and I fell into a deep sleep. Later, I woke up in the darkness of night, slipped out of my clothing and climbed into the sleeping bag, where I quickly fell asleep once more.

Day (15): 142 Km

July 22nd
Total 1442 Km

Tillebrook Provincial Park to Walsh

I did not wake until 5:30 am. the following day. I had slept (or been unconscious) for more than 16 hours, from midday and into the night, lying on top of my sleeping bag. Given the possibility that I may not have recovered consciousness, I wondered how long it would have taken before someone decided to investigate the little red tent under the trees!

I lay awake in the early morning light, thinking about the accident. I remembered the look of blank indifference on the face of the truck driver, who had merely glanced down at me, lying on the ground with blood on my face, before he revved his engine and drove away. In that awful moment, I experienced something that was different from the feelings of alienation and separation from others that I had felt in during the early days of this journey.

I remembered the look on his face, and I felt ashamed. I felt the shame of being seen as no more than discarded waste, lying by the side of the road, not worthy of a second glance. In his eyes I had become an object unworthy of attention or love and I could only hold myself and cry in the early dawn light, alone and forgotten in that small tent, far from anyone who cared for me. And then I remembered my children and the love that I had for them, my pain eased, and I returned to the silence of sleep.

Later, I woke and left that place. I cannot remember packing up the tent and my gear. I cannot remember how long it took before I left the campground or whether I paid before leaving or had paid the day before. I do not remember seeing anyone. I only remember cycling like a robot, slowly moving forward and continuing my journey to the east. Other than a general feeling of stiffness in my back and neck, I seemed to have survived my encounter with the potash truck and had returned to the road.

The mist cleared, and the sun rose above the horizon, like a great crimson fireball. I stopped the bike and gazed in silence, completely absorbed. I was grateful to be alive and the shame of yesterday forgotten. The morning air was cool and fresh, and the bike floated the 60 kilometres into Suffield, where I stopped for breakfast at a service station restaurant before heading toward Medicine Hat.

Later in the afternoon, my neck felt tight and painful, and I was forced to stop and stretch it every five kilometres to relieve the pain. Taking the turn off from the highway into Medicine Hat, I was feeling hungry once more, and my energy was fading. It was a long ride in the heat through the hills of the city before I came to the restaurant that I had visited with Jack the previous year. Once more, old memories of our trip returned, but I was hungry and paid them little attention as I devoured my late lunch.

I was back on the road before 3:30 p.m., and then, about five kilometres past Medicine Hat, the front tire collapsed with a loud bang. I could see that it was beyond repair, with a split down the side, and I needed a new tire. I sat by the side of the road and contemplated my predicament. It was obvious that the nearest place to purchase a new tire was back in Medicine Hat. The problem I had to solve was how to get there!

I stood beside the road and tried to hitch a ride in my usual manner, but there was little traffic, and any cars that passed ignored me and failed to stop. I realized that even if they had taken pity on the poor old bloke in distress, their vehicles would have been too small to carry me and the bike. I started to walk back to Medicine Hat. Eventually, I reached a picnic area by the side of the road, where I encountered a white-haired elderly couple, munching on potato chips and sandwiches. Following a brief discussion, during which I explained my predicament, they kindly agreed to look after my gear and the bike until I returned from Medicine Hat with my new tire. I was anxious to move on and so our conversation was short and to the point. However, I did wonder what they were doing, spending their afternoon sitting by the side of the TransCanada Highway with their large mobile home, but decided to ignore the question and simply accept with gratitude and trust that they were there and were willing to help me.

I removed the wheel and stood by the roadside. I was not sure if it was the wheel that I was holding out or the presence of the elderly couple, but within ten minutes, a car stopped, and I got a short ride back to Medicine Hat, where I purchased a cheap tire at a Sears store before hitching back again to the picnic area. I quickly fixed the tire to the wheel in record time, thanked my two elderly guardian angels, and resumed my journey to the east.

It was now 6:30 p.m., and I was feeling tired, hungry, and continuing to experience the physical effects of the accident. But I was determined to make up the time I had lost because of the tire problem and decided to head for a commercial campground outside Walsh, another 40 kilometres down the road. In retrospect, considering the significant bang to my head that I had experienced the day before, this was not the most balanced decision that I could have made!

Shortly before 9:00 p.m., the light was fading, I not eaten since early afternoon, my energy was low, and Walsh was still a distance away. I was riding into a strong wind blowing directly into my face, making it hard to think, let alone see the road ahead. Gradually, becoming more exhausted, I finally reached Walsh just before 10:00 p.m., only to discover that the campground was closed for the season.

I stood before the campground gate, reading and re-reading the notice. I wanted to erase this message of rejection. My mind was numb, my body exhausted, I was hungry, my water was gone, my neck ached, but I refused to leave. I knew that I had to find somewhere to camp. I could not go back into the growing darkness and face that fierce wind again, with no idea of where I would sleep that night.

The road was silent and empty, no pedestrians, no sign of life other than a faint blue light coming from a service station in the distance. It was my only hope!

Moments later, I pushed the door open and entered the station. I slowly walked up to a middle-aged woman with a long, sad face, who was sitting behind the service counter. No doubt due to my strange appearance, and coming in from the highway late at night, she looked at me with apprehension. I knew that I had to provide a convincing story if I was going to obtain her help. I explained very slowly the problem that I had encountered and asked if I could camp on the spare ground to the side of the building. There was a moment of hesitation, and then she looked into my eyes, saw the fatigue and desperation, and said that it was okay.

After thanking her profusely, I purchased a bottle of water, a large packet of potato chips, and a warm cheeseburger, that I immediately consumed, and then went back into the darkness and the wind to set up my tent on the service station lot.

There were no witnesses to observe my valiant efforts in the flickering lights, as I struggled in the darkness to push the tent pegs into the rock-hard soil. The wind increased in strength and, within minutes, had covered the tent with stringy brown tumbleweed blowing in from the nearby fields. I raced from corner to corner of the tent, attempting to secure all four corners. First, one corner would blow out from a half-hammered tent peg and then another. Finally, I solved the problem by weighting the tent down with small concrete blocks that I found scattered around the service station. Relieved that I had managed to avoid sleeping in the open, I finished the task, clambered back into the tent, and collapsed on top of my sleeping bag. I remember lying there, looking up at tumbleweed shapes outlined on the tent roof by the light from the service station. Grateful that I was warm and safe, I quickly fell into a deep sleep.

But the day had not finished with me! Sometime during the night, I woke to hear heavy rain pounding on the canvas roof of the tent, and immediately, I knew that I was in trouble again. I had been so tired in setting up the tent in the wind and darkness that I had forgotten to put up the fly sheet. I knew that it was only a matter of time before this heavy rain would penetrate the canvas and start to leak into the tent. Reluctantly, to say the least, I went out into the cold, wet night. I was naked, standing in the rain and howling wind, illuminated by the neon blue light of the service station sign, the darkness all around, and my only companions a crowd of crazy dancing tumbleweeds: it was indeed a traumatic spectacle, had anyone been there to witness it!

Husky Service Station Campsite

Finally, my task completed, I gratefully crawled back into my tent, dried off with a towel, and burrowed deep into my sleeping bag. Once more, brought to my knees by cruel fate, but still undefeated on my journey, I surrendered to sleep!

Day (16): 34 Km

July 22nd
Total 1476 Km

Walsh to Maple Creek Provincial Park

Woke early to the sound of trucks and vehicles on the highway outside the tent. I quietly and quickly packed up my gear, washed up in the station restroom, and then had breakfast in the restaurant. I had a headache, my neck was still sore and stiff, and so I decided to call it a day and head for Maple Creek, 34 kilometres down the road, where I could rest and recover from the stress of the previous two hard days on the road.

I arrived at Maple Creek Provincial Park, 34 kilometres down the road, somewhere around 9:30 a.m. I was feeling tired and lethargic. After setting up my tent on an isolated campsite, sheltered by small trees and low-hanging branches, I lay on my sleeping bag in the sun, feeling anxious and lonely. I must have fallen asleep or passed out for an hour or more before waking. I felt irritable, vulnerable, and did not want to be seen by anyone, so I retreated into the tent and lay down.

I began to think about the encounter with the truck driver, who had glanced at me with curiosity and then drove on, leaving me lying by the side of the road like a piece of discarded waste. And I remembered another incident in my life when I had felt ashamed and alone, reduced to being seen as an object of curiosity instead of a human being needing care and attention.

"I was five years old, and I could read. Every morning, I would make my way to school by taking a carefully prescribed route to a point where a crossing guard, dressed in a bright orange jacket, helped the children to cross over the road in safety. I always obeyed instructions and followed this route every day, except on Tuesdays, when I purchased a weekly comic called "The Beano," which I obtained from a newsagent, on the other side of the main street. I knew that I was forbidden to cross over the road by myself, but I had learned that, if I waited patiently, I could attach myself to groups of adults waiting to cross over.

One Tuesday morning, I was late for school, but I was determined to obtain my comic. Instead of waiting patiently in my usual place for adults to cross over the road, I saw that the traffic had come to a halt behind a small bus that was unloading its passengers. With a quick glance down the side of the bus, I stepped in front of it and started to cross. And suddenly there was a moment, a second of frozen silence, when I glimpsed the face of the truck driver staring down in horror, eyes wide open, as he saw the small child on the road below him. I remember this huge roaring beast with radiator grill teeth, thick rubber tires, and a gleaming metal bumper bar, bearing down on me.

And then I disappeared into a timeless, peaceful place. I felt nothing, no fear, no confusion, no threat, just an empty silence before I was pulled or dragged out of the blackness. I opened my eyes. I was lying on my back, looking up at a circle of adult faces in the sky above me. I felt no pain. I had no fear. I only knew that I had been pulled from underneath that truck.

But what I remember most clearly were the eyes of those adults, who stood in a circle in the sky above me. I remember their blank passive faces, and shiny eyes filled with curiosity, as they looked at the crumpled little body lying on the ground in front of them. No one was saying anything. No one moved to break the silence until I heard a voice shouting, "Move back, give him air to breathe."

Then strong hands lifted me from the ground. I was held close to a warm body and carried to a nearby doctor's office. I remember how that doctor, poked and prodded, asked questions and looked for injuries, but he found nothing, not even a bruise. I do not know or understand how I was run over and dragged from beneath such a huge truck and not sustain an injury of any description. I have always been grateful for my escape, but I will never forget the faces that looked down at me as I lay upon the ground."

I lay alone in that tent, reliving these feelings of shame and separation. I wondered why my childhood memory could still evoke such intense and difficult emotions after so many years. But I was tired and eventually gave up on my ruminating, turned over onto my side, and slept throughout the afternoon and into the evening.

Somewhere around 6 p.m., I woke up feeling groggy and confused. Eventually, I stirred myself and began searching the area around my campsite for twigs and small branches to make a fire for supper. Although I was not feeling very hungry, I ate supper, and then walked around the campground, spoke to no one, and finally went to bed.

Day (17): 130 Km

July 24th
Total 1606 Km

Maple Creek to Swift Current

I woke early, out of the campground and on the road before 6:30 a.m. The sun was shining, the temperature cool, and I could feel a slight wind blowing in my face. It was perfect cycling weather, and it remained that way for the rest of the day. With a soft wind at my back, and feather-duster clouds floating across a blue cathedral sky, I cycled on my way.

Entranced by the rhythm of the bike and the music of "The Nylons," I danced with the road, swinging along, singing aloud, no one to hear me, just living in the moment, just living the experience of the day!

The day was fresh born; I felt alive and connected to everything I could see around me, as I cycled through the fast, shape-shifting shadows of that open prairie landscape. I listened to Dvorak's "New World Symphony" and cried at the second slow movement. I felt sensitive, open, and vulnerable and became absorbed by thoughts of life, of the purpose of life and it's meaning and ending. Thoughts passing through my mind like meteor showers as I moved forward on the road to Swift Current.

I stopped for breakfast at a highway service station around 9:00 a.m., and then returned to the highway, where I quickly slipped into the sensitive open awareness that I had experienced earlier in the day.

Silently swooping along the hard shoulder of the road, I surprised perky gophers sitting on brown dirt mounds, alert for hawks swooping down from above. My giant shadow fell over them, creating a moment of fear, before small brown bodies dived into dark burrow mouths. Black crows gathered in gossipy groups, protesting at the intrusion created by my passing, before rising in noisy formation to escort me to the edge of their territory. Once more, I felt connected to the land, this space, that I was embracing as my own, on this long journey to be with my children.

Prairies Images

Prairie images imprinted upon my mind: sculptured cloud shadows floating across a vast landscape; splintered cries of hawks flying high above; patterns of light and shade reflected in pools of ancient water. I stopped the bike and stood in silence, feeling connected to everything that I could see and hear.

By late afternoon, the wind had increased from the north, and the sky was overcast with dark, heavy clouds that carried the threat of rain. The bright light and mystical mood of the early morning slipped away as I pedalled on spinning wheels, like a hamster on a treadmill, across a vast and timeless prairie landscape.

On the final stretch into Swift Current, I began to feel bored with riding alone along an endless highway, reaching a campground, setting up camp, cooking food over a small fire, sleeping and then waking to start the whole routine over again. I wanted to leave the road and escape for a while. I wanted to do something normal, like going to a movie, sitting back in fat plush seats, eating popcorn and being entertained. But without the prescription glasses, that I had left behind in a distant campground, I would not be able to see the movie screen. And so, my fate was sealed, and I could only move forward, each day blending into the next, condemned to ride this road forever, no movie breaks for me!

Off the highway and into Trail Campgrounds, Swift Current, around 5:00 p.m., where I quickly set up the tent, cooked supper, and climbed into bed before a heavy thunderstorm arrived. Sheltered under the trees, protected from the rain, feeling warm and secure, knowing that tomorrow would be a new day, I drifted off to sleep.

Day (18): 141 Km

July 25th
Total 1747 Km

Swift Current to Besant

I left the campground before 6:00 a.m. The weather was cool, and the riding was easy. Somewhere around 9:00 a.m., and about 50 kilometres down the road, I pulled into a Husky service station and consumed a huge breakfast, consisting of two large bowls of porridge, sausage, eggs, hash browns, bacon, and four rounds of toast!

Feeling tired and lethargic, as though I had not slept well (or possibly had eaten too much!), I cycled along, listening to my music. I had the road to myself, and then two young guys passed me. They were dressed in bright shirts and natty cycling shorts, riding light sprint bikes, spinning past in silence, leaving me plodding along the road like a tired old donkey." Rude young fellows," or words to that effect, I muttered to myself as they went past; they could have been polite and said hello to an aging fellow cyclist!

I stopped for lunch in Chaplin, where I purchased food supplies for the evening meal. The last part of the day passed with pain and drudgery. My backside felt sore, and keeping my seat on the bike was difficult. However, I had been able to maintain a better than average speed over the ten hours since leaving Swift Current, more than 140 kilometres away and arrived at the campground in Bessant at 4:00 p.m.

I checked in and found the same campsite that I had shared with my friend Jack on our journey west. How could I have imagined that within twelve months, I would be returning to Toronto on a bicycle and camping on the same spot? I set up the tent and checked out the campground facilities, which seemed adequate and then wandered back to my tent. I was feeling lonely and decided to phone Jack from a public phone on the highway outside the campground. However, when I got to the phone, I discovered that I did not have enough change to make the call! Jack accepted the charge, and we talked and reminisced about our trip and my experiences on this return journey by bike.

The connection with my old friend had improved my mood, and I was no longer feeling so bored and lonely. Cooked my evening meal (another delicious large can of Campbell's Vegetable Soup, no less!), retired into my tent and was asleep before nightfall.

Day (19): 93 Km

July 26th
Total 1840 Km

Besant to Regina (Holiday Wheels Campground)

I woke before 6:00 a.m., showered, and departed the campground before 7:00 a.m. The riding conditions were difficult, with harsh winds blowing in from the southeast. It took three hours of head-down hard riding to reach Moose Jaw, 30 kilometres down the road. Parked the bike beside the restaurant window where I could keep an eye on it and staggered into the main dining area. No one paid any attention to my arrival, and I quickly located a seat where I could keep an eye on my bike and gear. Glancing out of the window I saw the little red flag, that I had attached to the bike, fluttering in the wind, looking lively and ready to go, but I felt exhausted and discouraged that it was only 10:00 a.m., and I was ready to call a halt to the day.

Breakfast consumed, I reluctantly left the nice warm restaurant, and climbed back onto the bike to resume the ride into the wind, hour after hour of mechanical, repetitive motion. And then the wind eased, and the riding became easier as the day progressed.

Gradually, I became resigned to the monotony of the day, listening to music and simply observed the thoughts passing through my mind. At one point, I slowly cycled past the body of a deer lying on the hard shoulder of the road. I stopped and looked down at the clouded eyes in her cold corpse and wondered if my physical being would look like this poor animal, once my soul, my spirit, my life had departed from my body.

Riding, always riding and asking questions. Why am I here? What is the purpose of life? Why do we suffer? Asking aloud, but there was no one to hear, only the wind blowing into my face and scattering my questions to the universe.

I could feel the pain from my accident in Vancouver, pain from the crash into the potash truck, pain increasing in my right ankle and foot. To endure and accept this pain became a constant struggle, demanding that I stop every few kilometres to stretch and rest. Later, I sat by the side of the road, ignoring the curious looks from the occasional car or truck driving along the highway, as I munched on a lunch of apples, bananas, and granola bars.

I arrived at The Holiday Wheels Campground in Regina in the mid-afternoon. It was a terrible campground that primarily catered to large recreational vehicles set up on concrete pads. I had to pay $9 for my miserly bare dirt campsite, but the campground had a laundry and fine-looking showers, which enabled me to justify the cost.

I quickly set up the tent and lay inside on my sleeping bag and slept for the rest of the afternoon. At 6:30 p.m., I woke and walked over to a Husky service station restaurant, located just outside the campground, where I ordered steak and chips together with double helpings of bread-and-butter pudding, just like my Mum used to make!

And then, feeling much better, no doubt due to bread-and-butter pudding therapy, I ambled back to camp and settled in for the night hoping that tomorrow would be an improvement on the drudgery of today.

Day (20): 235 Km

July 27th
Total 2075 Km

Regina to Moosomin (Provincial Park Campsite)

I was awake before 5:00 a.m. and climbed out of the tent, feeling eager and ready to start the day by having a nice hot shower, only to discover to my intense chagrin, that the campground washrooms were locked.

My early morning enthusiasm evaporated, as I vainly rattled the washroom door and disturbed the early morning peace with choice words. Muttering to myself about the exorbitant campsite fee I had paid to have a hot shower, I packed up in disgust and left the campground.

As soon as I hit the highway, I felt the pressure of a strong west wind on my back, pushing me forward. Gradually, I moved the bicycle gears up to the top and began to skim across the road surface, pushing myself faster and faster. Encouraged by this powerful west wind speed, I set an ambitious goal of reaching Moosomin, more than 200 kilometres to the east, before the end of the day.

I remember the exhilaration, as I flew along the open road, wind at my back, listening to my music, rocking and rolling in the saddle to the pounding rhythms of The Gipsy Kings and Diana Ross. The drudgery of yesterday and the disappointment of the locked showers now forgotten, my pain was forgotten. I raced past prairie grain silos, strange statues of giant moose and Indian heads, standing silent by the roadside, oblivious to my passing.

Indian Head

I lost all sense of time during that ride on the highway, between Regina and Moosomin. I know that I briefly stopped for breakfast and later for lunch at service station restaurants along the way. I do not remember what I ate or how long I spent in each place. I only know that I had been seduced by the siren call of "The Magical West Wind," and, despite ravenous appetite and constant thoughts of food, my only desire was to return to her embrace without delay.

Prairie Grain Silo

Propelled like a rocket along the TransCanada Highway, I arrived in Moosomin before 6:00 p.m., and checked into a Provincial Park Campground, where I made sure that the washrooms would be open in the morning at an early hour! And after setting up my campsite and eating my evening meal, I strolled around the campground and met two guys heading west: Bruce, who was travelling to a new job in Thunder Bay, and Fred, who was hitch hiking his way to British Columbia. Later in the evening, they yelled for me to come over and grab a beer. I drank two beers, shared biking stories, and then returned to my campsite.

My face was sore from the sun and wind, my neck was still painful. I had pain in my left leg and hip area, but all things considered, I decided that this had been an exceptionally good day to be riding a bike across Canada; and with that thought I fell into a deep dreamless sleep.

Day (21): 160 Km

July 28th
Total 2235 Km

Moosomin to Brandon (Happy Valley Campground)

I woke before 6:00 a.m. and packed up slowly in the early morning light. The campground was silent, and no one was awake to witness my departure. Only the imprint of my body in the grass remained to mark my time in this place.

The weather was cool and sunny. Once more, aided by the strong west wind, I picked up speed and, in less than two hours had cycled the 37 kilometres to Elk Horn. I arrived with a monstrous appetite. Unfortunately, it was early Sunday morning, and none of the restaurants were open for breakfast. And so, with a famished determination, I set out again, leaving Elk Horn behind, searching for food along the way.

After riding for an hour, I passed a church set back from the road; the doors were open, and people were coming out. Ten or more of them were lined up at a mobile truck, buying packages of something. By now my hunger was intense and my food detectors were twitching. I had a sudden intuition that they might be purchasing food, and so I stopped the bike, parked it under a nearby tree, and joined the line.

I could not see the contents of these packages, and so I asked the woman in front of me, standing in the line, if she knew what was in them. I received an odd look before she responded, with what I mistakenly thought was a swear word! "Perogies," she said, which left me no wiser! However, a subtle but obvious smell of something edible was coming from these packages, and I did not care what they were since the good church folk in front of me were buying them by the dozen. I was hungry and so I also purchased a bag of these strange prairie perogies.

Food now in hand, and appetite raging, I jumped back on the bike, tucked my bag of perogies into the front saddlebag, and rode away. I wanted to keep to my schedule and decided to ride and eat at the same time. Leaning forward in the saddle, one eye on the road, I snatched the perogies from my saddlebag and savagely bit down, swallowing the little creatures in ravenous chunks.

It was not until I had eaten about five or six of them that I became aware of a strange floury taste. It was a taste that I had not noticed in my urgent need to get food into my stomach. It was a moment of insight. A moment when I suddenly realized that whatever "perogies" might be, I had just eaten the uncooked version! I stopped eating and tucked the bag away for later consideration, noting that at least I was not feeling hungry anymore!

With the wind at my back, I made fast time along the empty highway on that Sunday morning. I stopped at Virden, 30 kilometres down the road, and bought fruit and bottled water. Somewhere around 4:00 p.m., feeling very tired and with low energy levels, I saw a huge hill in the distance with a campground located at its base. Although I had not yet obtained food for my evening meal, I checked into the campground, set up my tent and slept for an hour.

I woke with a powerful appetite, and like a hungry bear, roused from its winter cave, set out to climb the steep hill and make the 20-kilometre round trip to Brandon, in search of a decent restaurant and a well-cooked meal.

I cycled about the downtown area and soon came across "Aunt Sarah's Family Restaurant," where I carefully read the menu on the door, and decided that chicken and chips, followed by raspberry pie and ice cream, would both justify the climb up the steep hill and compensate for my "perogy breakfast." After the meal, I freewheeled down the hill to the campground and made a cup of tea before retiring for the night.

Day (22): 168 Km

July 28th
Total 2403 Km

Brandon to Newquay Provincial Park (16 km East of Portage)

I woke at 6:30 a.m. and was on the road an hour later. It was a cool but dry day, and the cycling was easy. Just before 9:00 a.m., I came to a service station restaurant, where I obtained breakfast and was back on the road again before 10 a.m.

After an hour of steady riding with little or no wind to assist me, I was held up by road construction for five minutes. I cycled past an extremely attractive young lady holding a stop sign, who smiled and thanked me for going slow. I decided not to tell her that I had been going slow for more than two thousand kilometres, but I did appreciate the smile that she gave to me!

After cresting a steep hill, I began to glide down a long stretch of road. Looking down into the valley below, I could see a farmhouse with a long dirt path leading to the highway. I heard dogs barking in the distance and paid no attention until I got closer and saw a pack of them running down the path from the farmhouse. It took a moment, before it dawned on me that I was the object of their attention, and they intended to arrive at the junction of the path and the highway before I did.

Quickly, my survival skills honed to a fine edge after three weeks on the road, I switched into top gear and began to race down the hill, faster and faster. The sound and sight of the dog pack came louder and closer and I could see that, despite my impressive downhill speed,

I was going to "encounter" the pack, and I needed a plan of action to defend myself!

I suddenly had an image of myself playing polo, mounted on horseback, and wielding a long polo stick as I charged for the goal! And with that image in mind, I bent down, released the bicycle pump that had been strapped to the side of the bike frame, and let it swing out to its full length of about four feet. Loud and invigorating "Gypsy King" music was playing in my ears, and I was now prepared to defend myself! Balanced on my trusty steed, mind razor-sharp, and speed at full throttle, I flew past the junction, just ahead of the snarling pack.

Bicycle pump in hand, hanging low over the crossbar of the bike, I glanced down and saw the big black pack leader, teeth bared, mad gleam in its eyes, about to lunge at my right ankle! With a smooth swooping movement, I swung the pump and connected with his muzzle. There was a loud yelp, and he stumbled into the path of the other dogs. Suddenly, the pack was falling over each other, yelping, and crying in a state of disorganised chaos before coming to a halt on the side of the road. Glancing back and seeing the mayhem and confusion that lay scattered in my rear, I felt like a medieval knight, who had battled against overwhelming odds and emerged victorious!

Afterwards, cycling on down the road, I felt quite heroic and cheered up by this encounter!

However, notwithstanding the invigorating effect of my dog pack victory, my energy began to fade as the day went by. I stopped for lunch at a service station restaurant on the highway. Sitting alone, I paid no attention to the other customers in the restaurant. This way of life, eating at restaurants, camping, cooking, sleeping, and riding a bike hour after hour, had now become my life and familiar daily routine, and I realised that I was now fully immersed in this experience of 'journey."

Outside Portage, I repaired a flat tire in record time, climbed back on the bike, and suddenly felt a very sharp pain in my right ankle. By the time I arrived at a service station restaurant, shortly before Portage, the pain had become severe, and I could not exert any pressure on the right pedal. I thought that I may have strained the Achilles tendon in my right foot and was concerned that I may cause severe damage to the tendon if I continued cycling that day. And so, after picking up food supplies in Portage, I slowly and carefully peddled into a commercial campground on the highway and set up camp for the evening, hoping that the problem would simply go away.

However, despite taking anti-inflammatory medication, the pain kept me awake until well after sunset. I lay in bed wondering if it would be gone in the morning and concerned that it could prevent me from continuing the journey. Threatened by pain and anxious thoughts, piling up like a log jam in my mind, I fell into an uneasy sleep.

Day (23): 80 Km

July 29th
Total 2483 Km

Newquay Provincial Park to Winnipeg

I woke at 7:15 a.m. I had not slept well because of the pain in my ankle. I felt anxious and concerned that this pain was becoming more intense and could bring an end to my journey. But I was alone on the road, knew no one to turn to for help, and had to keep moving forward.

After packing up, I was on the road at 8:15 a.m. I kept to an easy low gear and applied only limited pressure on my ankle, but the pain did not ease. Every yard gained as I moved forward, each downward thrust upon the pedals, was paid for in the currency of pain.

Apart from this new and very painful condition in my right ankle, my hip was still painful from the encounter with the potash truck. Constantly moving and applying pressure, hour after hour cycling along the road, the aches and pains were increasing. My neck hurt. My face was now quite sun-burned, and I felt tired after pedalling for just a brief time.

Eventually, I stopped to rest by the side of the road and concluded that I had to halt my journey long enough to recover from the injury to my tendon and to regain energy. I also needed figure out my next move if the tendon did not heal and I was unable to ride the bike. And then I remembered that I had a friend in Toronto, Barbara Maslowsky, whose parents lived in Winnipeg, and I decided to reach out to her for help.

We had been in contact before I left Vancouver, and I knew that that she had told her parents about my intention to ride a bike across Canada. I wondered if they would allow me to stay with them for a day or two so that I could rest and assess the problem with my Achilles tendon. Three kilometres down the road, I found a pay phone outside a service station and called Barbara, who told me that her parents would be willing to help me and that I should call them when I reached Winnipeg to obtain directions to their home.

Around 12:30 p.m., I reached the outskirts of Winnipeg, found a pay phone, and spoke to Sam (Barbara's father). He confirmed that Barbra had called and that I was welcome to stay with him. He then provided directions to meet him at a junction on the road into the city.

It was a difficult ride through the city, with my ankle and hip pain increasing with each kilometre. It took two hours of hard and painful cycling to reach the assigned meeting point. I concluded that Sam did not ride a bike and therefore had not realized, when he selected our meeting point, just how long it would take me to get there.

In the distance I could see a pickup truck in a restaurant car park by the side of the highway, that fitted the description Sam had provided over the phone, and a feeling of relief passed through my poor old body.

I slowly cycled across the car park toward the truck.

"You must be Tom, I presume." said the stocky older gentlemen, standing by the side of the truck.

"Thought you might have got lost on the way, but it looks like you can't go too fast with all that lot to carry" he said, pointing toward my gear.

After shaking hands and exchanging a few pleasantries we climbed into the truck and set off for Sam's home.

Riding in the truck, bike and gear in the back, chatting to Sam as though I had known him all my life, I felt the powerful emotion of connection. And so, once more, on this long journey to be with my children, I experienced the kindness and generosity of strangers and learned that I do not have to find my way alone.

Day (24 -25): REST DAYS

July 30th – August 1st
Total 2483 Km

The Maslowsky Home in Winnipeg

I will never forget the care and attention that I received from the Maslowsky family. Evelyn, Sam, and Debbie (Barbara's sister) were warm, generous, kind people who welcomed me into their home and treated me like some kind of hero.

The next morning, I went with Sam to the local pharmacy, where I purchased an athletic bandage for support and anti-inflammatory gel to reduce the discomfort and pain. By the second night of sleeping in the luxury of a real bed, sufficient rest, and decent food, the pain had diminished to the point where it was hardly noticeable anymore.

On the morning of the third day, I was sitting in an exceptionally soft and comfortable chair, copy of the Winnipeg Sun in hand, waiting for a cup of tea to arrive, when I realized that I had adapted to the comfort of the Maslowsky home, and in the process had forgotten about my journey and the demands of the highway. The pain in my ankle had not completely disappeared, but I felt restless and anxious that, if I waited too long, I would lose the motivation to continue my journey.

I thought about the delay that had already taken place, the distance that remained, the commitment I had made, and decided that I must leave the comfort of the Maslowsky home and return to the road. I knew that there was a risk that my ankle could become inflamed and painful again, but I would not know if I could continue without getting back on the bike and setting off on my journey again.

By the time I had finished my cup of tea, I had decided that I would take it easy during the first days of cycling to gradually build up strength and hope that the pain did not return. If the pain returned, then I would have to discard the bike and hitch-hike and/or catch a bus to Toronto. I knew that this was an all-or-nothing strategy, but I could not wait any longer!

After supper, we played cards, and I told Sam that I would leave in the morning. We laughed and talked about our lives and the journey ahead. Later, lying in my comfortable, warm bed, I thought about the thousands of kilometres that remained before I reached my destination. I remembered the road, with day after day of cycling. I remembered endless repetitions of the same movements, moving forward, constantly moving forward and I felt discouraged. But then I thought about my commitment to this journey, and my children waiting for me to rejoin them; I heard their voices calling out to me from the open highway and my courage returned.

Day (26): 100 Km

August 2nd
Total 2583 Km

Winnipeg to Pine Tree Campground (35 km West of Falcon Lake)

After a leisurely breakfast, we placed the bike and gear into the back of Sam's truck and left the house. Driving out to the Winnipeg perimeter ring road, making conversation with Sam, I had the sensation that I was in a dream and would wake up any moment. It was hard to believe that I would soon be alone once more on the highway. We said goodbye, and Sam left. I stood standing by the side of the road, traffic streaming by, going into Winnipeg, and remembered the moment after Gordon had left me standing on the highway in Coquitlam. I quickly turned to check my equipment, found that it was all there, and resumed breathing.

I remember the stiffness and discomfort during those first kilometres heading east along the TransCanada Highway. Once more I started to experience pain in my lower back. My ankle was pain free, but I was afraid that the stiffness in my ankle meant that the inflammation had returned, and I would not be able to continue. Anxious thoughts, and emotions all clamoured for attention, but I ignored them, listened to my music, and cycled on. And with each repetitive movement, with each turn of the wheels, the pain diminished, time dissolved, and I became one with the bike again.

The hours passed by, and I lost awareness of the road, the motion of the bike, and even the discomfort in my body. I was only aware of my breath and the gentle music of Kitaro. Cool southern winds caressed my face, and I was back home again on the road. Later in the day, the wind in my face increased in strength, and I had to struggle, pushing harder to maintain any speed. Stopped for lunch at a service station and purchased food for my evening meal. Shortly after 4:00 p.m. I cycled past Pine Tree Campground, a small campground, located 35 kilometres before Falcon Lake. The place looked quiet and secluded, and I liked the name, so I decided to camp there for the night.

After supper, I sat beside a small stream, by my campsite, listening to the soothing music of it's fast-flowing water, and thought about my concerns. I could feel the stiffness in my ankle, but the pain was hardly noticeable, which hopefully meant that it would eventually disappear altogether and not slow my progress. I was confident now that could cycle on, but I would have to go slower. I knew that this would put me behind schedule, but by now I had become a more flexible and adaptable individual, than the one who had departed Vancouver, nearly 2600 kilometres and four weeks earlier.

I missed my new friends and the soft, warm bed in Winnipeg, and wrote a brief thank you letter to Sam. Then I settled into my hard bed to dream of soft feather pillows and a well-sprung mattress, waiting for me a mere 2000 kilometres down the highway.

Day (27): 114 Km

Aug 3rd
Total 2697 Km

Pinetree Campground to Longbow Lake (Heritage Place Campground) Kenora

I left the campground before 7:00 a.m. My ankle was sore and painful for the first hour or so but gradually eased as I cycled along a new and smoother section of the highway. Cycling into Falcon Lake, I encountered a heavy thunderstorm; a veritable deluge poured down from above and suddenly my world was filled with huge warm raindrops, and thundering trucks, throwing clouds of dust-clogged water spray into my face. I decided to increase speed and get out of the rain and these miserable road conditions.

And so, with heavy rain falling, and bright yellow poncho billowing out behind me, I swooped into The Falcon Lake Golf Club Restaurant for a well-earned breakfast.

Despite my trusty yellow plastic poncho, the heavy rain had soaked my feet and run down my back. However, I managed to dry off with towels in the restaurant washroom. My feet were wet and ached after pushing hard on the pedals for three hours, and I decided that in the future, I would protect them from the rain by taping plastic bags around my ankles, which I thought was quite an innovative solution to my problem. Given that my general appearance was more than a little unusual, I assumed that this new addition to my cycling outfit would blend in nicely and not be noticed!

No doubt the inclement weather had discouraged the local golfing fraternity from turning up for an early morning swing at the golf balls because I had the restaurant to myself. I took one quick look at the menu and saw that I could not afford my usual gargantuan meal, and so, after a modest breakfast of coffee, toast and eggs, I quickly departed.

The rain had stopped by the time I left Falcon Lake and at 11.45 a.m., on the morning of August 3rd, I reached the Ontario border! I stopped and ate my sandwich lunch on the grass beside a huge welcoming sign. The road was empty, and I had time to think and reflect on the struggle and pain, the peaceful and the joyous moments, that I had lived before reaching this significant point on my journey. Although I still had almost 2000 kilometres to ride, I had passed over the border into the province where my children lived and where I had spent so many years of my own life, and I knew that I had entered the final stage of my journey. Afterwards, I took a photograph of the sign, climbed back on the bike, and set off for Kenora.

A Large Welcome Sign

I arrived in Kenora at 5:30 p.m., and slowly made my way through the town. It was a holiday weekend with heavy traffic and tourists crowding the sidewalks as they shopped for happy memories. I ignored them all, quickly purchased food supplies for my evening meal, and left the busy place behind.

After an hour of steady cycling, the dull pain in my ankle became sharper, and so I decided to find a campground and call it a day. I pulled into the Heritage Place Campsite, located about 16 kilometres east of Kenora, around 8 p.m., and slowly set up camp beside a small RV with a young couple named Bob and Moira, heading to Calgary.

After cooking and consuming my usual canned supper, I was invited over to their campsite, where I drank three rye whiskies and a beer, entertained my new friends with bike riding anecdotes, and then tottered off to bed in a slightly inebriated state.

During the night, I woke to the sound of rain pounding on the roof of the tent and noticed that the roof and sides were starting to sag inward. I realized that the ground outside the tent had become wet and soggy, causing the tent pegs to loosen and the tent to sag inward, threatening to collapse in a cold, wet pile on top of me!

Muttering at the injustice of it all, I climbed out of my nice, warm sleeping bag and into the rain. I was sleepy, naked, being eaten alive by mosquitoes, and feeling very vulnerable. A repeat performance of a dark and stormy night, more than a thousand kilometres and two weeks ago, beside a service station in Walsh! And once more, the performance was enacted entirely for the benefit of the local insect population, as they buzzed with appreciation for the show that I was putting on!

I banged the tent pegs deeper into the ground, and quietly contemplated the fact that, apart from being attacked by huge blood-sucking prairie mosquitoes, everything I owned was either damp, wet, or cold! Back in the tent, all secured and safe once more, consoled by the thought that life on the road is only for the brave and the bold, I faded into a dreamless sleep.

Day (28): 120 Km

August 4th
Total 2817 Km

Longbow Lake to Dryden (Birchland Trailer Park)

7:00 a.m., and I lay awake, looking up at the tent roof and deciding what to do. The pain in my ankle was gone, but I was concerned that it would return once I was back on the road. To stay or to leave was the question to be answered. Keeping as much of my body as possible in the warm sleeping bag, I stuck my head out of the tent and saw dark skies, heavy with rain. I felt unmotivated to repeat yesterday's rainy ride and decided to take it easy, rolled over and went back to sleep.

I slept until 10:30 a.m. and woke when the rain stopped. Clambered out of the tent, showered, ate three raisin buns and a small can of fruit cocktail, packed up my gear, said goodbye to my convivial friends from the night before, and was back on the road before midday.

I had previously noticed that the tensor bandage supporting my ankle, had left deep marks in the skin, and so I decided to loosen it to see if that would reduce the pain. After riding for about an hour, my ankle felt more comfortable. I then experimented by gradually increasing speed and found that I could do so without increasing the pain in my ankle. After an hour or so of steady cycling, I remained pain-free, and so, encouraged by this positive change, I cycled on, feeling stronger, moving forward once more.

I stopped for lunch at a roadside restaurant just west of Vermillion Bay and realized that I was now back into my nomad life on the highway. The comforts of Winnipeg fast becoming a lovely memory. I was once more living each day, one day at a time, with the end destination a mere reference point in a distant future. However, coming into Dryden at 7:00 p.m., any fanciful notions that I had discarded the comforts of civilization in favour of the spartan glory of the open road, began to fade.

I was tempted by seductive visions of soft sheets and a comfortable bed in a warm motel room, complete with all the conveniences required to renew and nourish a weary middle aged bicycle rider. But filled with resolve not to weaken, I thrust the temptations aside and turned into a trailer park/campground, checked in, and set up my tent beside a huge RV parked on the next campsite.

That was when I met Wilber and Jenny, my new next-door neighbours in their huge RV. I had planned to ride into Dryden and find a restaurant for supper, but when Jenny found out about my intentions, she insisted that I join them and their 13 friends for supper.

I was no longer preoccupied with concerns that the pain in my ankle would get worse and threaten to end my journey and as a result my mood and general outlook had improved. I told stories, laughed and joked all evening with a crowd of people that I had just met, and then, feeling happy, connected, and well fed, I wandered off to my own campsite around 10.45 p.m., and went to bed.

Day (29): 101 Km

August 5th
Total 2918 Km

Dryden to Ignace (Berglunds Camp)

Once more, I woke up to rain pounding on the tent roof. The jolly camaraderie of the previous evening forgotten, I turned over, buried my face inside the sleeping bag, and went back to sleep again without even checking the time.

Eventually, I got out of bed and showered. Started chatting to Dot and Bill of the BMW Biking Group, based in Wisconsin, who invited me to join them in Dryden for breakfast. Dot, aged 62, told me that she had ridden more than 300,000 miles on her motorbike, which made my little journey seem quite insignificant.

Breakfast finished, new friends and conversation left behind, I was back on the road at 10:30 a.m. The day was cloudy with occasional drizzle and quite cool. I felt tired and low on energy, but it was not a hard ride, and I was in no hurry to get anywhere. The morning passed easily, cycling along an empty road that turned and twisted through the green forest. I felt discouraged at the prospect of spending another night inside a cold, damp nylon tent and once more considered taking a motel room for the night. Reached Ignace around 5:30 p.m. and made inquiries at The Westwood Motel. However, I quickly dropped the idea when I found out that it was $29 plus tax for the night. Eventually, I came across a commercial campground just outside town and decided to treat myself to a restaurant meal as a consolation for giving up the comfort of a nice warm motel bed.

Day (30): 109 Km

August 6th
Total 3027 Km

Ignace (Berglunds Camp) to Upsala (Inwood Park Campground)

I woke early and was on the road at 6:30 a.m. The day was clear and sunny. After two hours of steady cycling, and no restaurants in sight, I stopped the bike by the side of the road and snacked on fruit and nuts for breakfast.

Later in the morning, I met a young woman in her mid-twenties, heading west. The road was empty of traffic, and we could see each other from a distance, gradually getting closer and closer. Eventually, we stopped on opposite sides of the road. She looked fresh, energetic, well-rested, and well-spoken. In comparison, I felt grubby and not so attractive! She told me that she had set out from Montreal and was going to Vancouver. She also described herself as a "free camper" who camped out of sight in the woods, instead of campgrounds. I thought that she was very brave but wondered how she managed to look so fresh and clean without access to hot showers and laundry facilities.

After she left, I stood alone by the side of the road, feeling older and more alone in my life than I cared to admit, and watched her disappear into the distance. Would I always be alone, always feeling this nagging anxious awareness at the back of my mind? I forced the thought away, climbed back onto the bike and applied myself to the task at hand.

The day was one of the best riding days of the journey. Apart from one or two hills just beyond Ignace, the road fell gradually all the way to Upsala. The weather was sunny and bright, with a light breeze and broken clouds dancing in the dark blue sky overhead. I gave myself permission to let go, no worries, just floating along, listening to music. I forgot about distance, why I was on the road, or where I was going.

I stopped for lunch at English River, where I treated myself to a fine meal at a large service station restaurant located on the outskirts of town. Standing at the counter placing my order, I joined in the conversation about the weather and listened carefully as other customers shared news about events and happenings out in the larger social world. I had previously noticed that I felt self-conscious in my biking gear and kept to myself when I stopped to eat in one of these roadside restaurants, but now it seemed I was quite willing to engage in conversation with other customers and restaurant staff. After a month on the road, I had assumed my new identity as an "old bloke on a bike."

In the late afternoon, I reached Inwood Park Campground, and selected an isolated campsite by the lake. It looked like a thunderstorm was coming, so I quickly set up the tent and cooked my evening meal before it arrived.

Lying on my sleeping bag and listening to the rain pattering on the tent roof, I felt safe and content. It seemed strange that earlier in the day, I had felt so lonely after meeting the young woman on the road, and now, although I was quite alone and had not contacted anyone in the campground, I felt content. Pondering the relationship between solitude and loneliness, I fell asleep.

Day (31): 122 Km

August 7th
Total 3149 Km

Upsala to Kakabeka Falls (Provincial Park Campground)

Got up at 6:00 a.m. and went for a swim in the lake. After the swim, followed by a good morning solid soaping that left me feeling refreshed, I quickly packed up and set out. On the way out of the campground, the chain broke. Not sure if I could fix the problem, I pushed the bike to the highway, where I hoped to find help if I needed it.

At first, I had no idea of how to solve the problem and just sat by the road, hoping someone would stop with an offer to assist. But the drivers of the three cars that passed in the next half hour, did not seem to notice my presence. Eventually, I opened a small but well-packed bag containing a selection of bike tools, that I had randomly purchased from Canadian Tire before leaving Vancouver. I carefully laid out all the contents hoping for inspiration. And no doubt, it was more inspiration or luck rather than skill, but I did manage to use one of the gadgets to remove the broken link and reconnect the chain to the bike. It took the better part of an hour to solve the problem and be on my way again.

Listening to the music of Dvorak's New World Symphony, I quickly slipped into a pleasant, dissociated, state of mind. The road was wide and smooth, the wind behind my back. I was moving forward once more and feeling quite pleased that I had managed to repair the bike chain. However, this section of the highway did not have any roadside restaurants or service stations where I could stop for breakfast, and so I was forced to cycle on through the morning, munching on granola bars, held in reserve for such emergencies.

I arrived at Shabaqua around 12:30 p.m. and found a restaurant. Apart from the problem with the bike chain and granola bars for breakfast, the morning ride had been easy, but I had to wait an extended period before my breakfast was served. And as I waited for my food, my thoughts turned to my life, my children, my father's death, and my hopes for the future.

Then the food arrived and quickly abandoning my existential musings, I consumed double helpings of French fries with a double cheeseburger, followed by two generous helpings of blueberry pie, topped with double scoops of ice cream. Breakfast consumed, I sat quietly for a while sipping on my coffee and concluded that long-distance bike riders with immense appetites, will always choose food over personal and philosophical ruminations!

After leaving the restaurant, I had to climb three or four steep hills. This proved to be something of a challenge for a digestive system that was still processing such a large lunch! However, highway traffic remained light, with a car or truck passing every 10-15 minutes, and the cycling became easier as my body efficiently transformed carbohydrates into energy.

The long open expanse of the prairies left far behind, I was now travelling a different road, a ribbon of light cutting deep into the dark green forests and lake country of Northern Ontario. Tall trees bowed and whispered in the wind as I passed by. The quick, bright flash of butterfly wings flickering in the breeze, the monotone sound of insect choirs and the strange bell chimes of raven warnings, welcomed me to this place: I felt at peace and connected to the land and the life that surrounded me on the road to Kakabeka Falls.

Later, I thought of those long silent moments, moving deeper into the dark arboreal forests of Northern Ontario. I remembered the trees, pressing close to the road. I remembered a sense or feeling of being observed, of being connected to the life around me, and later, I wrote in my journal:

Dark shadows conceal
Beetled creatures woken from sleep
To watch with slivered eyes
The stranger dancing on the road
To the music of clicking pedals
And fat tires humming
I cycle past
Just being here
Now.

I arrived at Kakabeka Falls around 4:30 p.m., stopped at a service station convenience store, and purchased food for the evening meal, before checking into the Provincial Campground. I felt calm and peaceful from the afternoon ride and wanted to be on my own in the quiet silence of solitude. I selected a campsite away from any other campers, where I set up camp and prepared my evening meal. Later in the evening, I took advantage of the clean and efficient campground facilities to clean my grubby clothing and have a shower before retiring for the night.

Day (32): 115 Km

August 8th
Total 3264 Km

Kakabeka Falls to Wolf River Campground

I woke at 6:00 a.m. and was on the road an hour later with the intention of riding 30 kilometres to Thunder Bay where I planned to eat breakfast.

I reached the outskirts of Thunder Bay around 9:30 a.m. and encountered heavy traffic streaming into the downtown core along a wide, six-lane highway. Giant neon signs, endless concrete block warehouses, repair shops, and fast-food outlets lined each side of the road. Hoping to find a better restaurant to get breakfast, I ignored these first offers and pushed on into the city. The sun was relentless, and the temperature increased. I stopped the bike to apply more white zinc ointment to my face, ignoring the strange looks from commuters in passing cars, as they gazed upon this alien being from another planet, applying his war paint before entering their city!

After an hour of riding, I had not found anywhere to eat and regretted that I had not stopped at one of the fast-food outlets that I had seen earlier. And then, I noticed a tourist information booth attached to the side of a building, set back from the highway. I pulled over to inquire about restaurants in the city of Thunder Bay. Getting closer, I could see that the information booth was closed, but there was a broken "Hotel" sign attached to the door of the main building, and another sign in a window saying" Open."

I parked the bike, opened the door, and stepped back in time!

The room had an old musty smell that hung in the warm air, like a second-hand bookstore. I stood inside the doorway, my eyes adjusting to the daylight filtering through two small, curtained windows and a single light hanging from the ceiling. There were cheap plastic chairs and round metal tables, randomly scattered about an otherwise empty room. In the far corner, I could see an antique Coca-Cola fridge and an old lady sitting alone behind a wooden counter.

I waited a moment in the doorway before saying "Good morning" in a loud, cheery voice.

"No real meals dearie, only hamburgers," she said, pointing to a chalkboard hanging on the wall behind her head.

I moved closer to get a better look and saw that there were three varieties of hamburgers listed. I ordered two cheeseburgers, which she noted on a small pad, before turning to walk through a curtained door into what I assumed was the kitchen area.

When she returned, I purchased a large bag of potato chips that I gobbled down while waiting for the main course to arrive. After ten minutes, the cheeseburgers arrived, complete with condiments on a tin tray. They were terrible-looking creatures, but I was so hungry, I wondered if I should have ordered three!

After eating my food, I ordered a coffee and conversed with the old lady, who told me that her name was Magda, and she was the owner of the hotel.

"The hotel's best days are gone now," she said. "Been here since 1933 but the traffic all goes by now."

She lived alone in the back of the hotel with her cat, named Horace. She also employed an elderly gentleman named Harold, retained from the days when the hotel was a thriving business, who came in every day to cook the hamburgers. She told me about the days when Thunder Bay was known as Fort William before it amalgamated in 1970 with the nearby town of Port Arthur to form the city of Thunder Bay.

"Things have never been the same since, "she said.

Food eaten, conversation ended, I purchased three donuts and rejoined the highway traffic, heading east through the city. Within ten minutes and less than a kilometre down the road, I came to a service station restaurant and grocery store. And if I had known it was there, I could have dined on pork pie and chips instead of soggy old cheeseburgers, but I would have missed my encounter with an interesting old lady, marooned in a dilapidated hotel, telling stories from the past to ageing bike riders, who wander in from the highway.

Once I was clear of Thunder Bay, I decided to press on toward Nipigon, another 120 kilometres down the road. I had no expectations of reaching Nipigon that day but thought I might find a campground on the way. Around 2:00 p.m., I stopped to eat two ham and cheese buns that I had picked up at the grocery store in Thunder Bay. By late afternoon, feeling tired, my energy level low, and legs made of lead, I came to Wolf River Campground and rode in to check it out.

I joined a line of vehicles waiting to gain admission to the campground and began to chat with a woman and her two children. By the time we got to the check-in gate, we had arranged to take adjoining campsites and continue our conversation.

And that is how I met Sandra and her two sons, Bron and Brian, aged 8 and 11 years old. The campground was excellent, with great showers and a fully equipped laundry room. I had planned to set up camp and then head back along the highway to pick up food from a roadside service station, but Sandra invited me to supper with her children. We had beef stroganoff and rice, which was most enjoyable. After supper, we sat and talked, sharing details of our lives and getting to know each other, before I said goodnight, and feeling happy to have met this lady and her two boys, returned to my campsite and settled in for the night.

Day (33): REST DAY

August 9th
Total 3264 Km

Wolf River Campground

I woke at 6:15 a.m. and decided to go fishing in a small stream that flowed past the campsite. I had discarded my fishing pole because it had become inconvenient to carry, but I still had the line, hooks, and sinkers, so I decided to try my hand and see if I could catch something.

I slipped quietly through the dew-soaked grass to the stream, and remembered my childhood, when I caught fish by using a small twig as a float, a piece of ham as bait, and a small weight to sink the line. It worked then, so why not now, I thought?

Stepping onto a rock in the middle of the stream, I let the line sink and watched the twig, hoping that the current would carry the bait to hungry fish waiting for their breakfast. Suddenly, I felt a slight tug on the line, a moment of hesitation, and then again, another tugging sensation. I let the line run for a moment, and then, not knowing if I had just caught a snag under the water, I pulled it in to discover that I had caught a small brook trout!

Having mastered what was obviously a proven fishing technique and confident that more fish were in the stream, I placed my catch into a plastic bag and proceeded to catch seven more, before a fine drizzle of rain began to fall. Flushed with success, I returned to camp: the hunter-warrior returning with food for the tribe no less; unfortunately, no one was yet awake to witness my triumphant return!

The Hunter-Warrior on The Job

The rain stopped around 10:00 a.m., and the campground came alive with the sound of voices and cooking pots, which was the signal for me to emerge from my tent to display the morning catch to admiring eyes. Sandra seemed impressed that I could ride vast distances on a bike and live off the land at the same time!

Later in the afternoon, we all went river tubing, returning to the campsite as a light rain started to fall. Dressed in Sandra's orange raincoat and looking like a dishevelled school crossing guard, I cooked the evening meal for my newfound family. A magical moment, caught on camera for posterity!

Later, we talked over a glass of wine and shared more intimate details of our lives. Sandra talked about her marriage and the problems that she and her husband were experiencing. I spoke of my children and the journey that had commenced, more than 3,000 kilometres to the west, to rejoin them.

At the end of a very civilized evening of tasty food, wine and pleasant conversation, I returned to my tent, where I lay quietly in my sleeping bag, listening to faint voices talking and laughing in nearby campsites, and light rain falling on the canvas roof over my head, before falling asleep.

Day (34): 105 Km

August 10th
Total 3359 Km

Wolf River Campground to Rainbow Falls Provincial Park

I woke at dawn and heard the familiar sound of rain falling on the tent roof, before turning over and going back to sleep. The rain stopped at 8:00 a.m., and I struggled out of my sleeping bag, showered, packed up the tent and gear, ate breakfast with Sandra, and prepared to leave.

We hugged goodbye and agreed to meet up later in the day at Rainbow Falls Provincial Campground, just over 100 kilometres down the highway. Half an hour later, heavy rain began to fall. Cycling along, protected by plastic bags on my feet and yellow plastic poncho, I sang and felt happy on the way to Nipigon, where I arrived at midday, found a restaurant for lunch and used the washroom to change into dry clothing.

The rain had stopped, and it was close to 3:00 p.m. before Sandra caught up with me, 20 kilometres past Nipigon. I had another solid 60 kilometres of riding before I would arrive at the next campground in Rainbow Falls Provincial Park, where we planned to meet up again. To make the ride easier and faster, Sandra took my tent, equipment, and heavy panniers with all my belongings, and the race was on!

The ride to Rainbow Falls was spectacular. Without the heavy weight of the tent and equipment, I felt unleashed and powerful. My speed was impressive as I hurtled along the road, powered only by the strength in my legs and a light following breeze. I would like to have met up with those young guys, back on the highway, dressed in their snazzy pants and riding light bikes, who had rudely flashed past me without saying hello; I would have taught them a lesson or two about manners and bike riding!

The scenery was spectacular, with green forests and immense lake views shimmering in the distance across the gleaming waters of Lake Superior. I climbed uphill with ease and swooped downhill, fast falling like a hawk diving for prey. Released from the burden I had been carrying for so long, pounding fast along the flat stretches, I whooped and hollered. I was racing in the Tour de France; the finish was in sight, and I had left the pack far behind!

And then I came to Muffin Hill! Although I was riding without the additional weight of tent and equipment, I was unable to climb this steep hill, the first of three very steep hills that I would encounter on the highway around Lake Superior. The wheels kept slipping in the deep, loose gravel of the roadside, forcing me to dismount and push the bike to the top. I had no idea where the name came from, but I could have benefited from a couple of bran muffins to turbo-charge my climb to the top of that monster hill!

Muffin Hill

I arrived at Rainbow Falls Campground at 6:00 p.m., having cycled 60 kilometres (including Muffin Hill) in less than three hours, which I thought was good going for an old bloke from Stoke (my hometown in England)! I quickly located Sandra and the adjacent campsite that she had reserved for me. She had already eaten, so I made a campfire and cooked myself a meal of soup, buns, and canned fruit. Later, after the two boys had vanished into the camper van, we sat around the campfire with a glass of wine, talking long into the evening before retiring to our respective campsites.

Day (35): 90 Km

August 11th
Total 3449 Km

Rainbow Falls Provincial Park to Neys Provincial Park

I woke at 7:15 a.m., showered, packed up the tent and equipment, and then joined Sandra and the boys for breakfast. After a long leisurely meal, we made plans to reconnect in Toronto, and then we said goodbye. I left the campground around 10:00 a.m. The day was clear and sunny, and I made fast time into Terrace Bay, arriving just before 11:30 a.m. I was feeling hungry and was easily lured into a bakery by the smell of fresh bread and other delights. Once inside, I purchased a dozen butter tarts for $1.59., and promptly devoured them all sitting at a roadside picnic table outside the bakery.

I had not seen Sandra and assumed that she had driven past while I was preoccupied with gobbling down my butter tarts. However, half an hour later, as I approached a small hill, I had an intuition that we would be meeting at the top. At the top of the hill, I stopped and waited. Within two minutes, she appeared. We talked for a while and then said goodbye. She was going to move faster now, and we would not meet on the road again. Feeling the return of a familiar sense of loneliness, I cycled on.

That night, I camped in Neys Provincial Park. The campground was superb. I loved the beach and felt at peace there. After my evening meal, I sat outside the tent and looked over the water. It was moment of quiet reflection, in which I sensed the passage of time, not just the time that had elapsed since I left Vancouver, which seemed a lifetime ago, but also the time passing on this greater journey of my life. I remembered my life when Michelle was a small child, and Sean was a baby. It was over ten years ago, and yet it seemed like yesterday. And I wondered if long-distance bike riding, of being immersed in the experience of "journey," may change our awareness of time passing and influence the subjective meaning of our lives.

By now, it was 9:30 p.m., and the light was fading, hot water was steaming for tea, and the campground table was cluttered with unpacked equipment and dirty pots. I knew I had spent a very enjoyable time with Sandra and her boys and had not thought about returning to my solitary journey and the demands of my life on the road. Once more I was alone, but this time I felt comforted by the connection and the time I had spent in Sandra's company.

Although I would not arrive in time for Sean's birthday, I wanted to be in Toronto before the 21st of August. He would be playing his first soccer game on that date, and I wanted to be there to support him, which meant I had to plan my days to achieve that goal. But I no longer felt the need to maintain the single-minded determination and purpose that had marked the early days of my journey. I knew that it was all going to work out fine.

And so, feeling grubby, warm and sticky, I decided to leave my shower until the morning and quietly climbed into my sleeping bag.

Day (36): 150 Km

August 12th
Total 3599 Km

Neys Provincial Park to Obatanga Provincial Park

I woke early feeling ambitious. My plan for the day was to ride to Obatanga Provincial Park, located 150 kilometres east of the campground. The weather was cool and clear with no sign of rain or high winds, and I calculated that by maintaining a steady pace I could reach my destination before 8:00 p.m. I knew from my trip by car the previous year that the road to Obatanga was level, with no steep hills to slow me down, and so I thought that my goal was quite reasonable.

I left the campground just after 7:00 a.m. with the intention of eating breakfast at one of the restaurants located on the highway junction leading into Marathon. However, when I arrived at the junction, somewhere around 9:30 a.m., they were all closed. I did not want to make the time-consuming round trip into the downtown area, and so I decided to ride on, hoping to find an open restaurant further along the highway. I had "emergency granola bars" which guaranteed that I would have something to eat until a restaurant turned up.

About 20 kilometres past the Marathon junction, I noticed a car in the distance. It came closer, slowed down, and stopped on the opposite side of the road. I slowly cycled up to it and saw two people in the vehicle: a middle-aged driver and a younger woman sitting beside him.

The man called out to me, and I heard the concern in his voice, as he said,

"Thought we should warn you that we saw a huge black bear feeding in the bushes by the side of the road back there.'

It took a moment or two before my dissociated brain figured out what they were saying and what, if anything, that had to do with me. We looked at each other for a moment, and then I asked,

"Did you see any bear cubs?"

Which was the only intelligent response I could think of at the time!

"We didn't see any cubs." He replied. "But they could have been hiding in the bushes."

Having warned me of the impending danger that lay ahead, they wished me luck and drove away.

The sound of their departure faded into the distance, and the silence of the surrounding forest returned and once more I was alone and vulnerable. I sat on my bike and let the information sink in. I knew that my trusty bicycle pump technique, previously employed to fend off a marauding pack of farm dogs, would not be successful in fending off an angry 500-pound mother bear, intent on defending her cubs. On the other hand, I could not just sit on my bike forever waiting for inspiration.

And so, decision made, and no clear plan in mind to deal with the threat ahead, I set off in the direction of the danger, hoping that I would produce an effective strategy, if a bear should appear.

I remember my intense focus as I peddled along that empty highway, anxiously scanning the edges of the forest. At one point, whilst I was deep in a bear-searching trance, peddling as quietly as possible, there came a great shrieking cry on my right side, and I nearly fell off the bike with fear. It was a purely reflexive reaction on my part and no doubt the same for the large black crow, who had been quietly eating his breakfast by the side of the road, when my uninvited, gigantic presence flew right over his head!

I slowly cycled on, pondering the possible outcomes that lay ahead. And then I remembered my granola bar emergency food rations, and I had an idea: I could throw the granola bars into the path of any charging bear, distracting its attention away from me and, as it snuffled after my food, I would be able to make a quick getaway!

I was under no illusions about the limitations of this hasty plan, but it was the best that I could do under the circumstances. And so, for the next 20 minutes, a mental struggle took place on that lonely forest road: I could either eat the granola bars to satisfy what had now become a ravenous hunger or save them to distract a large angry bear. With each passing kilometre, and no bear in sight, I began to convince myself that, with or without cubs, it had moved back into the forest.

And so, with that fine piece of logical reasoning in mind, I reached into the front bag, hauled out a granola bar, chomped down hard, pushed on the pedals, and left the ursine threat behind.

Breakfast finally arrived in the form of two ham and cheese buns and a couple of apples purchased from a roadside store on the highway. Not a satisfying meal but, combined with the granola bars was sufficient for my needs.

On the road to White River, I came to a long steep hill that I did not remember from my trip west; no doubt because at that time I was going downhill in a car and not riding uphill on a bike loaded down with camping equipment. It was a difficult climb, one that had caught me by surprise, and I could see that it was going to slow my progress.

But I accepted my fate, pushed down hard on the pedals and gradually toiled up that steep incline, every now and then lifting my head to keep the hilltop goal in sight, and then pressing down hard once more, never giving up, determined to reach my goal. The effort to keep going, not to dismount became more and more intense and strangely familiar. At times I could feel tears streaming down my face, but I did not know why. And later, resting on the hilltop by the side of the road, I remembered and relived an incident from my childhood:

"I was six years of age, and it was sports day at St Mary's Primary School. I was competing in the sack race for small boys. I remember the slippery grass surface of the playing field and the white chalk lines stretching into the distance, marking the lane that I had to follow. I remember the effort as I pushed hard, toes jammed into the corners of a burlap sack, driving forward, grunting with effort. Ahead, I could see my father holding the finish tape. I heard other boys on each side of me, all breathing hard, each one striving to beat me, to reach him before I did. And as I dived first over the line, I heard someone say,

"Did you see the look on that boy's face, Michael? That boy was very determined to win the race."

Pushing hard, grunting with the effort, I climbed that hill into White River and cried for my father, knowing that all I ever wanted was his love and attention. I remembered my determination to reach him. And now, on this journey, pounding down on the pedals, I have experienced the same determination and single-minded purpose to achieve the goal of reaching my children. Pounding down, one leg after the other, pounding hard onto the pedals of the bike, the finish line ahead, my father holding the tape, my children waiting for me, I struggled up that hill with the aid of this forgotten memory.

Other memories came back to me as I sat on that hilltop by the side of the road. Memories of my father sitting alone at the dining room table, reading the Sunday paper, smoking a cigarette. We did not converse together, share thoughts, or talk about concerns. But I felt close to him in those silent moments. During my early and adolescent years, I had wanted his attention, and tried to become the man he wanted me to be but then he died, and I stood alone upon a stage, my lines forgotten, the audience gone.

After returning to Canada from his funeral in England, I became depressed and lost all sense of purpose and direction, particularly with my business career. I became afraid, and fell into a deep emotional pit, as I struggled to understand his death and the meaning of death in my life. Questions of meaning, life and existence clouded my thinking, and I became lost in the darkness of my mind.

And then, one day, standing in the living room of my apartment in Montreal, as I was trying to explain my fear and confusion to my wife, I left my body and looked down upon myself. I could both see and hear myself talking, and then the moment ended, and I abruptly sat down. It was a moment of clarity. I knew that I had to change, to find a new direction and in that moment, as I sat upon the living room couch, I decided to become a psychologist.

This was not a rational decision based on such things as research, study and evaluation. But it was such a clear insight that I immediately felt calm, my depressed state of mind disappeared, and my thinking became clear and purposeful. The decision made that day shaped the next ten years of my life as I obtained the required undergraduate and graduate degrees that would eventually lead to my registration as a clinical psychologist.

Questions of meaning and purpose have become my companions on this journey, as they have been at every stage of my life. Searching for answers, writing, endlessly writing, I wonder who will read my words and what meaning will they find in this tale of my journey and my purpose in making it.

Later in the afternoon rain began to pour down from heavy dark clouds. I donned my yellow poncho, fastened the plastic bags on my feet, and cycling hard arrived in White River at 6:30 p.m. I still had another 40 kilometres before reaching my goal of Obatanga Provincial Park and decided to eat my evening meal in a restaurant on the highway at White River, hoping that the rain would ease off while I was eating.

I quickly finished my meal and hit the road around 7:30 p.m. The rain became heavier, and the wind began to thrash into my face. I had to remove my sunglasses in the fading light and had difficulty seeing the road ahead. After two solid hours of hard cycling, I had still not reached Obatanga and could not gauge how much further I had to ride. I started to feel afraid and stopped the bike. I stood by that roadside in the dim forest light and pouring rain, trying to calm my mind. Once more, I found myself alone on my journey, lost and separated from those that I loved.

And then Ernie appeared in his pickup truck! God bless his cheerful, helpful soul! He came into my nightmare like an angel sent to rescue me; a lost and lonely waif standing by the roadside in the fading light and pouring rain. There was not much to say as we drove the four kilometres to the campground. I think he could sense my tiredness and allowed me to remain quiet, but I felt his kindness and compassion, and I was grateful that he had stopped to help a stranger on the road.

I pushed my bike past the dark and empty gatekeeper's hut and found an empty campsite. Once the tent was up and my gear stowed away, I stumbled down a slippery gravel path to the camp showers, hoping to get warm and dry my wet clothing in the laundry room. The door was unlocked, and no one else was there to witness my relief and yodelling pleasure, as familiar hot and soapy water eased my chilled body and calmed the fear in my mind.

Body warmth restored, clad in dry clothing, I emerged from the showers into a black night. There were no lights on in the campground, and I did not have a flashlight. Once more, in the dark and the rain, I could not find my campsite. Feeling miserable, blundering around in the rain, my feet getting wet, my dried clothes getting wet again. The light from a passing truck finally helped me to find my site.

I crawled into the tent, discarded my wet clothes, and hid under the sleeping bag, eating potato chips in the dark. Warm shower forgotten, feeling sorry for myself but grateful that I was no longer abandoned on the highway, I slowly went to sleep, thanking God for small mercies!

Day (37): 135 Km

August 13th
Total 3734 Km

Obatanga Provincial Park to Lake Superior Provincial Park

The sound of rain drumming on the tent roof woke me at 6:30 a.m., I thought about returning to sleep, and even turned over, closed my eyes and waited for oblivion to return. But I was getting too close to my destination and my mind was restless with the urgency of reunion; so, I got up.

I showered, shaved and managed to dry all my wet clothing in the laundromat, before leaving the campground at 8:15 a.m. The clouds parted, the morning light streamed through the treetops, and I was ready for another day on the road. Ten minutes after leaving the campground, Ernie appeared, this time heading west. He turned his truck around, and we spent time together, chatting and laughing, like two old mates who had known each other for years, instead of mere hours.

Planned breakfast was a light snack (two butter tarts, egg sandwich, and an orange) purchased from a service station convenience store. With food in the bag, I cycled on, looking for a place to stop and eat and came across a small, silent lake, away from the road, where I sat quietly listening to the wind and sounds of the forest. By the time I had eaten breakfast and returned to the highway, the wind had changed direction and was now blowing strongly into my face from the north.

It was approximately 40 kilometres to Wawa and then another 80 kilometres to Rabbit Blanket Lake Campground, my destination goal. The traffic was light, and I kept my head down, listening to music and allowing thoughts to just float through my mind without paying them much attention.

Michipicoten Hill, just before Wawa, was a long uphill ride that left me feeling tired. After a short ride down the far side of the hill, I came across an authentic old-time grocery store, with thick wood plank floors and tiny windows, which must have supplied provisions to the original settlers. I purchased $17 worth of groceries from this fine establishment, together with a detailed map of the provincial parks and lakes along the highway around Lake Superior, and then returned to the highway to resume my journey east.

I arrived at Rabbit Blanket Lake campground in the late afternoon. Set up camp and met Norman and Les, who were driving west to Vancouver from London, Ontario. Cooked and ate a very hearty supper of vegetable soup, followed by a precooked chicken concoction, and two cans of fruit. I had intended to head off to bed after the big meal, but Norman and Les invited me over to their campsite for a beer.

Halfway through my second beer and in the middle of a conversation on the relative merits of ice hockey and basketball, I suddenly experienced a rumbling discomfort bubbling up from somewhere deep in my intestines. With a mounting sense of panic, I made a mumbled excuse and rapidly headed toward my campsite and then into the woods! I don't know how long I staggered around in the undergrowth, groaning, and trying to obtain relief from the discomfort.

Eventually, after discarding a significant number of unwanted calories, and trying to be positive about the event, I concluded that I was now becoming an expert on the relative effects of various food combinations and their impact on the digestive systems of long-distance bike riders; hard earned knowledge indeed, and no doubt something I could investigate in more detail with a future research paper on the subject!

Day (38): 130 Km

August 14th
Total 3864 Km

Lake Superior Prov Park to Pancake Bay Prov Park

Woke early, around 6:30 a.m., showered, and packed up. Leaving camp, I met Norman and Les, returning from what they described as an "inspiring" early morning walk. I carefully refrained from discussing my rapid departure from their campsite the night before but did mention that there were times when I could have used a bit of inspiration myself!

The weather was calm and clear with little wind and the promise of a warm day ahead. I felt relaxed and decided to maintain a steady pace, aiming to cover the 130 kilometres to Pancake Bay Provincial Park without having to push myself too hard. About three kilometres past the campground, I stopped for breakfast and sat by a lake where I consumed three cream cheese and tomato rolls left over from yesterday's food supplies.

Lakeside Rest Stop

Writing notes by the lakeside, munching on my breakfast rolls, with the warmth of the early morning sun on my face, I was reminded of peaceful times from my childhood, sitting by the side of another lake:

"It was early morning, and I was the only one awake. I quietly moved through the silent house, my little fishing rod in hand. My two brothers were asleep in their beds, and I could hear the whistling rumble of my father's snoring coming from behind the closed door of the big bedroom. Carefully opening the front door, I stepped into the empty street and stood for a moment in the silence of the day, when only small children, with fishing rods in hand, were up and about their business.

I was 7 years old, and I had discovered my own world on those early summer mornings, when the adults were sleeping, and the rules were forgotten. At the end of the street, I climbed over a high stone wall and into the locked and silent park. Keeping an eye out for park keepers on the prowl for recalcitrant little boys, I took the pathway to a small lake where I sat quietly for hours, eyes fixed on a tiny fish float, suspended on the dust-pollen surface of the lake."

I remember those mornings when I sat alone, drifting into silent mind, simply observing, content to be there, feeling safe and connected to the quiet energy that surrounded me.

And now, almost 40 years later and thousands of kilometres to the west on another continent, I sit beside a lake, once more drifting into silent mind, simply observing, content to be here, in quiet solitude, feeling safe and connected both to this place and to an earlier time of my life.

Ten kilometres past Montreal River, I came to another of the short steep hills, including Muffin Hill, that I had encountered on the highway around Lake Superior. After a hard climb, I stopped the bike, feeling hot and tired, and discovered a lake where I went in for a swim to cool off. I could see large round boulders below the clear sharp water of the lake. Later, I thought about the glaciers of the Ice Age, which had formed these steep hills around Lake Superior. Ice walls of unimaginable weight, kilometres high, carving out deep chasms in the hard rock strata of The Canadian Shield, creating steep hills and convenient lakes to cool down old blokes on bikes.

The rest of the day passed as though in a dream. The cycling was easy and steady, thoughts passing through my mind, music playing in my ears. I felt grateful to be alive and immersed in this experience of "journey."

Just before 7:00 p.m. I checked in to the campground at Pancake Bay and set up camp. I could not find twigs or branches lying around to make a fire for my supper and had to buy firewood at the campground store. I remember feeling most annoyed and disappointed that I had to pay $2 for a measly bundle of wet wood that would not burn easily. However, since I was a qualified first-class boy scout, who could light a fire on a rock in the middle of a stream with one match and no paper, a measly bundle of wet firewood should not be a big challenge. In fact, I managed to create a small bonfire from that wet bundle.

Pancake Bay Provincial Park

Supper cooked and consumed, I decided to take advantage of the public pay phone at the camp store and make a phone call to Toronto to speak to Sean, since today was his birthday. I spoke briefly to him, told him that I loved him and was planning to arrive in Toronto in time for his soccer match on the 21st. I then spoke to Michelle, who thought that I had been sleeping in motels every night. When I told her that I was sleeping in a tent, she exclaimed, "Bizarre," which both surprised and informed me that I would be returning to a more grown-up and sophisticated version of the young lady that I had left behind last year. I also spoke to Marg, who offered to meet me on the road outside Toronto and drive me into the city to avoid having to cycle through the heavy traffic entering the city.

Encouraged by her generous offer and appreciating the time it would save, I decided to spend a day on the beach at Pancake Bay and gather my energy for this last stage of the journey.

Day (39): REST DAY

August 15th
Total 3864 Km

Pancake Bay Provincial Park

I woke in the early morning light and remembered that this was going to be a rest day. And so, I pulled the sleeping bag over my head and returned to sleep until 8:15 a.m. Finally, motivated by the thought that other campers would use up all the hot water, I reluctantly climbed out of my nice, warm sleeping bag and set off for the campground showers to begin my day.

After my shower, I cycled down the road to a service station and purchased food for my breakfast. Returned to camp, where I consumed a breakfast of fried bologna and tomatoes on plain buns, followed by raspberry jam on raisin buns: enough to feed an army!

Later, in the afternoon, I slipped into the warm waters of Pancake Bay and dived deep to the bottom of the lake, where I retrieved three smooth and ancient stones, to keep as reminders of this quiet and peaceful place. I kept to myself all day, thinking about the ways in which this intense experience of "journey" was changing the ways that I thought about myself, my life and my relationships; both past and present

And as I was sitting in the warm sun outside my tent, memories of another journey came to mind: a journey I had undertaken when I was 20 years of age and decided to emigrate on my own from England to Australia, where I lived, travelled, and worked for three years.

"In 1962, Australia was a distant, exotic land that lay on the other side of the world. Communication was slow and tedious; telephone calls were booked three days or more in advance and to get there required a long sea voyage by passenger liner. But I wanted to leave England. I wanted to escape the familiar and the mundane. I wanted an adventure, to leave home and return a hero, especially for my father!

I felt trapped in a life that had become boring and predictable, with the prospects of an office job, beer on a Friday night, church on Sunday, and eventually a wife and children to go with the house and mortgage. I decided that I wanted to travel and see the world, to become something more than just another "Bloke from Stoke," my hometown in England. I wanted to leave and separate myself from everything and everyone connected to me and start a different life: a life of my own making!

And so, without discussing my plans, I made up my mind and simply informed my family that I was emigrating to Australia. This was a shock to my parents, and when they asked why I wanted to make a such huge decision, I merely replied,

"Because that is what I want to do with my life."

I remember in detail the day that I left my old life behind. My two brothers, two young sisters, mother, father, and I were tightly packed together in my dad's small blue Austin 10 sedan. We drove to the railway station, where I was going to take the train to London from there to Southampton, the port of departure for Australia. I don't remember if anyone said anything during that short ride. But I do remember that we stood on the platform making conversation and talking about anything, except the fact that I was leaving and would be gone for years.

The heavy clock, hanging like a full moon over the platform, was showing 12.15 p.m., when the London train arrived in clouds of smoke and steam. I hugged everyone, starting with my youngest sister and finishing with my dad, who shook my hand. And then, feeling only the rush of adventure and relieved that I was finally on my way, I climbed into the railway carriage, closed the door, lowered the window and looked out onto the platform to see my family, who loved and cared for me, huddled together in a small silent group. And then, as the train began to slowly move away, I leaned out of the window, holding up my hand in a victory salute until the train turned the bend, and they were gone.

I stood for a moment by the window, listening to the clattering rhythm of the train wheels as they increased speed. I cannot remember going to the washroom, but I do remember the long, silent moment, as I gazed at my face in that washroom mirror. I saw that little group standing close together on the platform, and I could not breathe. I felt tears running down my face and my heart felt heavy as I grieved for the loving family that I had left behind."

That moment and the image of my family standing on the platform haunted me when I was in Australia. I never forgot that moment of sad, lonely pain, as the train left the station, and realized that, in my search for adventure and excitement, I was leaving the people that I loved and who loved me.

Three years later, I returned to them with a greater appreciation of the love and connection that we all need to sustain us through this journey that we call life. And now, once more, I am returning to those that I love by making this journey.

The rest of the day was spent in quiet contemplation and solitude, remembering and feeling connected to the people I had loved, and who were no longer in my life, and to those that lived and loved me still.

Day (40): 160 Km

August 16th
Total 4024 Km

Pancake Bay to Thessalon

I woke in the deep silence of the forest.

Everyone in the campground was asleep. I quickly packed up the tent and gear and began to cycle along the campground road leading to the highway. I could hear campers waking to another day, and I wanted to shout out in a loud voice,

"Adios, I am going home!"

But I kept quiet and rode alone in the cool morning air, seeking the warmth of the sun and the open road ahead.

Ten kilometres past Pancake Bay, I coasted down a very steep hill and pulled into "The Agawa Trading Post," where Jack and I had stopped on our journey west. The steep hills around Lake Superior had been too much for my old Plymouth station wagon. With steam erupting from under the hood, we had been forced to pull into the parking lot of the trading post. I was afraid that our trip had come to an abrupt halt. However, the problem was simply a broken fan belt that we repaired at a nearby service station, so that once more the dynamic duo and their trusty steed were able to resume their journey to the west coast.

I sat on a bench under a large maple tree beside the service station and felt sad as I thought about the sense of adventure and enthusiasm I had shared with Jack as we drove west. My old Plymouth Station

Waggon has been destroyed, nothing lasts forever, and I still have far to go before my journey ends. And with that thought, I mounted my trusty steed and rode away, leaving those memories behind.

Half an hour later, out of the corner of my eye, I saw a silver light shimmering through the trees. I stopped the bike and discovered a small path leading to a quiet peaceful lake, where I ate the breakfast buns that I had picked up at the trading post. Breakfast consumed, I returned to the highway and, with the help of a strong west wind at my back, I reached the junction leading into Sault Ste Marie at 1:00 p.m. and found a restaurant, parked the bike and went inside to order lunch.

I had covered the 80 kilometres from Pancake Bay, including the breakfast stop by the lake, in just over four hours. Feeling quite pleased with my progress, I took a large and enthusiastic bite of a delicious, melted cheese and mushroom burger, and suddenly experienced the pain and unpleasant sensation of a tooth breaking apart. Glancing around to see if anyone was watching, I opened my mouth, wiggled my tongue around, and a tooth filling dropped onto my plate with a sharp metallic sound!

I was able to assess the situation very quickly. I knew that I could not continue the journey for another 700 kilometres with a gaping hole or worse in my tooth! However, I was still in the grip of a powerful lunchtime appetite, and so I continued to carefully chew on my delicious half-eaten burger whilst simultaneously pondering this new and unexpected dilemma.

Lunch consumed and with a plan in mind, I left the restaurant and rode back along the highway to a tourist information office that I had seen earlier. I carefully explained the nature of my problem to the helpful and sympathetic tourist officer and was able to phone a dentist located in the Sault Ste Marie downtown area. I explained my situation to the dental receptionist, who was able to provide me with an emergency dental appointment.

To save time I decided to hitchhike into the downtown area. I carefully concealed my chain-locked bike and gear behind a service station and quickly obtained a ride into town. Once in town, I picked up cash from a bank machine and presented myself and my cavity at the dental office. Forty-five minutes later and $45 lighter, with a temporary filling in place, I hitched back to the Husky service station, relieved that I had solved the problem so efficiently, and could now continue my journey.

But the bike and my belongings were no longer where I had left them!

I gazed at the empty spot where they should have been sitting patiently waiting for my return and felt a sudden strange mixture of fear and anger; fear that I was alone, vulnerable, and unable to move without my bike and anger toward whoever had stolen it!

Suddenly, a friendly-looking fellow, dressed in a grease-stained mechanics boiler suit, appeared from behind a parked car, heavy black spanner in hand and a big smile on his face.

"Took the bike and put it in the shop," he said. "Thought somebody might steal it. Must be a bloody heavy thing to ride,"

I thanked him profusely, got on the bike, and rode off quickly, not believing what had happened or, more to the point, what might have happened if the bike had been stolen!

Back on the road, the sun was hot, and my face was starting to burn. However, the wind was strong at my back, and so I headed for Bruce Mines another 60 kilometres down the road. Went through Bruce Mines just after 6:30 p.m. I was maintaining an average of 20 kilometres an hour and decided to take advantage of the ideal cycling conditions and continue to Thessalon, where I discovered an excellent municipal campground (Lakeside Park) located just off the highway.

By now it was nearly 8:00 p.m., and although the campground was open, there was no attendant on duty to allocate a campsite. I decided to take the initiative by selecting my own site, with the intention of paying the camp fee on my way out in the morning.

I set up camp, lit a fire, and ate a warmed-up can of "Irish Stew" with three buns, followed by a large can of fruit. Set off for the showers only to find the door locked. Because I had not checked into the camp, I did not have a key. I stood gazing at the locked door when a guy suddenly opened it on his way out. I wished him good evening and quickly stepped inside before the door closed.

It was dark by the time I emerged from those nice hot showers, and I was feeling pleased with myself at being able to get into the washroom without a key. But that smug feeling did not last long when I discovered that, once more, I had forgotten to bring a flashlight. It took a little while to find my campsite in the dark, but at least it was not raining.

Day (41): 120 Km

August 17th
Total 4144 Km

Thessalon to Massey Chutes Provincial Park

I was awakened at 6:45 a.m. by the raucous sound of blue jays screeching outside the tent, telling me to rise and go about my business.

I felt tired, no doubt a residual effect from yesterday's intense dental activity. I cycled slowly through the sleeping campground, past the closed and silent gatekeeper's hut and made my way to the highway and breakfast.

Five kilometres down the road and 20 minutes later, I realized that I had forgotten to pay my campsite fee. I considered returning to the campground and then wisely concluded that it was not my problem if park employees kept banker's hours! And with that fine piece of reasoning, I decided to treat myself to a big breakfast with the money I had saved.

I pulled into a service station restaurant at about 9:00 a.m. and ordered a double serving of hash browns with extra bacon and eggs, four slices of toast, orange juice and coffee. I sat waiting for my order to arrive and looked around at the three or four tables occupied by people eating breakfast and engaged in conversation with each other. I was surprised that my arrival, clad in skimpy cycling shorts with helmet in hand and sun-peeled face, had not attracted any curious attention. I also noticed that I no longer felt self-conscious or alienated from these people: no longer special, not even "an old bloke on a bike," I had become just another traveller on the road.

I returned to the highway at 10:00 a.m. The weather was perfect for cycling, with clear skies, sunshine, and a slight breeze from the west. I reached Blind River around 12.30 p.m. and decided to press on, eventually stopping around 2.00 p.m. at Serpent River Falls, where I had lunch at a service station restaurant.

After lunch, I went for a swim in The Serpent River and then slept for half an hour on the rocks by the falls. I had originally intended to aim for Espanola, which would have meant cycling 150 kilometres for the day. However, just before 6:00 p.m., I reached Massey Chutes Provincial Park, 30 kilometres west of Espanola and decided that I was too tired to continue. Pulled into the campground and checked in with the park gatekeeper, who told me to select a suitable site and then return to pay for it.

I cycled around the campground, found a campsite away from other campers, unpacked my gear and set up the tent. Walked over to the showers and discovered that the campground did not have laundry facilities, which was disappointing, since I was now feeling very grubby and beginning to smell. Despite the possibility that my personal body odour may prove to be less than inviting to others, I decided to yield to temptation, forget about cooking my evening meal and eat at a restaurant on the highway.

I cycled out of the campground, intending to pay the camp fee on my way to the restaurant. Unfortunately, I discovered that the gatekeeper had closed his hut and disappeared for the night. Concerned about any further erosion of my moral standards relating to campground fees and absent gatekeepers, I made a sincere mental note to pay the fee in the morning before leaving the campground.

Quietly slipping into the restaurant, I sat in a corner, separated from other diners and hoped that no one would notice any unusual odours that may seem to be originating from my table. Feeling relaxed and content with my day, I consumed a great but expensive $10 meal consisting of veal parmigiana, mounds of French fries and a double serving of rice pudding.

After my lovely evening meal, I slowly cycled back to the campground and climbed into my tent just as heavy rain started to fall. Ignoring the ambience in the tent, created by my unwashed clothing and good self, I lay awake thinking about the few days remaining before I reached Toronto, and my long journey would end.

Day (42): 145 Km

August 18th
Total 4289 Km

Massey Chutes Provincial Park to Rutter

I woke at 7:00 a.m., to hear the familiar sound of rain on the tent roof. Lying half asleep, buried deep in my warm sleeping bag, I thought of the day ahead. I wanted to get an early start, but I had not paid my campsite fee, and the campground office would not open before 9.00 a.m. I was facing a difficult moral decision: I could wait for the office to open, or I could leave early, gain distance on the road and have a fine restaurant breakfast with the campground money I had saved.

Two hours and 30 kilometres later, I reached Espanola, where I found a nice-looking restaurant, and got on with the business of consuming a splendid breakfast, whilst simultaneously promising to make a charitable donation to The Salvation Army in lieu of my campground fee.

My clothes were very grubby, and I was beginning to smell even more than usual. Once more, I positioned myself as far away as possible from other customers in the restaurant and hoped that my personal odour would be covered up by the breakfast smell of bacon and eggs drifting in from the kitchen. The need to find a campground with a laundry had now moved up to the top of the priority list!

Breakfast consumed, I returned to the road with the intention of leaving the TransCanada Highway, after Sudbury, and taking Highway 69 south to Toronto. The weather was cool and overcast, and I cycled along at an easy pace. Later in the morning, I located a payphone and called my friends Jack and Susan, who agreed to let me stay with them until I got settled into my academic program and found my own accommodation.

Around 1:00 p.m., it began to rain heavily; great fat globs of water poured from the sky and pounded onto my head and back. I stopped the bike, put on my yellow plastic poncho, tied plastic bags to my feet and continued to cycle toward Sudbury. About 15 kilometres east of Espanola, the front tire went flat with a loud explosive bang. I spent an hour by the side of the road in the pouring rain, crouched over like a deflated yellow balloon, trying to fix what I thought was a "puncture." Then, I discovered that the tire had split open along the seam. Muttering to myself about the "cheap" Chinese tire that I had purchased from Sears back in Medicine Hat, I packed everything back into place and stood by the road, bike at my side and a hopeful look on my face.

God bless the people who take pity upon wet and bedraggled cyclists standing helpless in the rain! After ten minutes I was able to obtain a ride into Sudbury with Bob and his niece Michelle in their pick-up truck. We reached the cut-off into Sudbury, and I realized with dismay, that once the tire was repaired, I would have to face at least an extra hour of cycling through heavy traffic to get back to the highway again.

We arrived in downtown Sudbury. I disembarked from the truck, said goodbye to Bob and Michelle and looked around. That was when I realized that it was Sunday and the majority of the retail outlets were closed. I also remember thinking that life on the road is obviously not conducive to keeping track of time or even knowing what day it is!

Feeling very dirty, scruffy and "a sight for sore eyes" as my dear Mum would say, I found a corner bench outside a hardware store and sat quietly, observing the trickle of pedestrians passing by on their way to a nearby church. I sat on that bench for ten minutes, quietly running assorted options through my mind.

Option one, I find a way to purchase a new tire today and then cycle back to the highway or option two, find a motel/hotel and wait for the stores to reopen for business tomorrow. But first, I needed more information and so I crossed over the road to a convenience store that was open, checked the yellow pages in the store phone book and obtained the address of the nearest cycle shop.

With a clear destination in mind, and with the slim hope that on the way I may come across a hardware store that sold bicycle tires, I left the bicycle locked to a bike rack, minus the back panniers with all "valuables," and set off on foot to find "Taylor Cycles and Repairs" on Elgin St, located approximately five kilometres away. Obviously, my brain was not functioning at full capacity because it did not occur to me to check that the cycle shop was open before leaving the store.

Walking down the road, traffic going by, carrying the panniers on my shoulder, I felt tired, but I was also relaxed and amused by the change of pace. I was continuing my journey on foot and even without a bike to pedal, nothing was going to stop my forward momentum. However, my good humour quickly evaporated in the heat and noise of the city. No trees, no silence, no view, no lake - Just fumes and traffic noise.

I walked along the city sidewalk feeling vulnerable and wondering if this five-kilometre hike may not have been the best strategy and I knew that I had to find another solution.

Then, I saw a large convenience store on the other side of the road that was open for business. I knew that convenience stores sold a product called "duct tape," sometimes known as "the wonder tape" capable of sticking or binding anything together. It was moment of miraculous insight. I could bind the tire with duct tape to construct a temporary tire patch. This would seal the split in the side of the tire, I could then pump up the inner tube and problem solved!

I quickly crossed over the road and into the store, where I purchased a roll of hockey tape, which I thought might prove to be even tougher than duct tape, and quite suitable for the manufacture of a temporary tire seal.

Back on the sidewalk and trudging back to where I had left my bike, I felt relieved, more in control of the situation, and suddenly hungry. Food consumption now at the top of the attention list, I stopped at an Italian fast-food outlet, where I rapidly consumed an exceptionally large bowl of spaghetti and plump little meatballs.

Half an hour later, I reached the spot where I had left my bike and was relieved to find that it was still there. I removed the back wheel, wrapped the hockey tape to support the side of the damaged tire, pumped air into the tire, switched the front and back tires, climbed onto the bike, and very carefully moved away. The tape held fast, and I had solved the problem of my split cheap tire.

It was now 3:15 p.m., and I decided to take my chances with my hockey-taped front tire. Instead of remaining in Sudbury overnight and finding a bike shop the next day, I thought that I could rely on the temporary seal until I could purchase a new tire from a bike store on the way to Toronto. And so, leaving Sudbury behind, I rode back to the TransCanada Highway, hoping to find a campground for the night.

And as the hours and kilometres went by, I became hypnotized by the whirring sound and flash of the hockey tape, spinning into sight with each rotation of the wobbling tire, and prayed aloud to the cycling gods to keep it in place!

By 8:00 p.m., the skies were dark and overcast with the promise of heavy rain. I was now travelling south on Highway 69 toward Toronto. I had maintained a steady average speed on a level road and had still not found a campground. But I had learned my lesson from past experiences and had no desire to be caught in the middle of nowhere again, riding a bike with a makeshift patch on the tire, lost in the rain and darkness of the night.

It was still light when I made the wise decision to stop, just outside Rutter, and ask for permission to "free camp" behind a Texaco service station. Permission granted, I set up my little red tent in a secluded area of the station lot without any of the problems that I had encountered on my last attempt to camp behind a service station. Although I had not yet found a place to clean myself and launder my clothing, I took advantage of the service station washroom to make myself "presentable" before entering the empty restaurant.

After my meal, I returned to my tent and, oblivious to the sounds of highway traffic and the lights of the service station, I retired for the night.

Day (43): 110 Km

August 19th
Total 4399 Km

Rutter to Parry Sound

I woke at 6:30 a.m. to the sound of heavy road traffic going past my tent, which meant that Toronto was not far away, and it would not be long before I would see my children again.

I quickly packed up and washed my face in the service station washroom before going for breakfast at the restaurant. On the road at 8:30 a.m. The weather was cool and cloudy, but no rain or high winds. I felt tired and concerned about the makeshift patch on a tire that continued to wobble and vibrate with each rotation. But I had survived the drama of Sudbury and had managed to return to the road and continue my journey.

At noon, I came to a roadside food stand. After a brief conversation with the attractive young woman who was operating the stand, and pleased that my general appearance, minus the white zinc warrior stripes, was not evoking curious stares from others, I purchased six freshly baked delicious blueberry tarts. Out of sight of the stand and the young lady, I gobbled down four tarts and saved two for later.

Somewhere around 2.00 p.m., it began to rain with heavy intermittent showers that lasted for about 10 to 15 minutes, forcing me to stop the bike, change into my rain gear and ten minutes later stop and remove them again. And then, the hockey tape started to come loose. I pulled over to the side of the road, re-taped the front tire, and continued to ride on through the rain. This performance was repeated twice that afternoon, but I was still moving forward on the road toward Toronto and that fact alone enabled me to cope with the frustration of this start, stop, and tape up cycle.

It was a boring, frustrating day cycling through the rain and increased traffic. By late afternoon, the rain had stopped and just before the cut-off into Parry Sound, I pulled over to the side of the road and considered my options. Toronto was close, and I wanted this journey to end. Even though I had to keep stopping, the temporary repair to the tire had been more successful than I had expected. I had lots of spare hockey tape, which meant that I would not lose time by leaving the highway in search of a new tire.

And this meant that I would be able to reach Toronto with one more day of hard cycling.

And so, with what seemed like a clear plan, I cycled into a commercial campground, just outside Parry Sound, and set up camp before heading for the showers and laundromat.

Feeling a new man, showered, shaved, and clothing nicely laundered, no longer surrounded by the unwashed fragrance of "Eau de Tom", I rode back to the highway and discovered a Pizza Hut outlet where I created an incredible pizza with more dressings and toppings than I had ever had on a pizza before; in fact a most memorable meal that could have set a new high for pizza toppings in the Guinness book of records.

Later in the evening, as the daylight slipped away, I lay quietly in the tent, hearing light rain on the roof and the faint whisper of voices from nearby campsites, and I thought about the ending of my journey, an ending that had been so difficult to imagine before now.

Day (44): 205 Km

August 20th
Total 4604 Km

Parry Sound to Richmond Hill (Toronto)

I woke feeling impatient and excited. It was 6:00 a.m., and I wanted an end to this long journey.

I remember feeling tired and uncertain as I tried to figure out a plan for the day. The outskirts of Toronto were now within striking distance, but I had to balance my impatience in wanting to end the journey quickly against the risks involved in trying to cycle over 200 kilometres with a hockey-taped tire. I knew that Marg's offer to meet me on the road and drive me into the city would reduce the distance I had to travel, but it lacked the trumpets and fanfare I had imagined would mark the conclusion of my epic journey. On the other hand, if I refused her offer, I would have to spend another night on the road, which was not very appealing now that I was so close to the end.

What to do, what to do? I began to feel like an imaginary character from Alice in Wonderland, rushing around with teapot in hand and going nowhere.

The weather was cool and cloudy and with a strong north wind at my back, and I made fast time into Port Severn, sixty kilometres north of Barrie where I stopped for breakfast. Somewhere along that stretch of road I decided that I would forgo the trumpets and fanfare of returning the triumphant hero; this was going to be my last day on the road. I decided that I would just keep cycling, trying to get as close to

Toronto as possible, where I would meet Marg, and the journey would finally end.

I remember cycling hard and fast, especially around Barrie where I connected with Highway 400, the main highway leading into Toronto. The traffic was heavy on this major eight-lane highway, and I began to increase speed along the wide shoulder, feeling more confident that I could reach the outskirts of Toronto before dark.

Suddenly, I heard loud shouts and bellows coming from the other side of the highway. I stopped the bike and saw an Ontario Provincial Police officer standing beside his police car. After the traffic cleared, I could hear what he was saying. He was yelling that I had been breaking the law by riding my bicycle on the highway and that I had to get off at the next intersection or he would arrest me, which I perceived at the time as being unnecessarily threatening. And then, with his warning delivered, he climbed back into his vehicle and sped away, no doubt being called to police more serious criminal matters!

Feeling irritated at this rude intrusion, I exited Highway 400 and began to cycle down Highway 11, still feeling annoyed that the police officer had disrupted my plans.

And as I cycled on, I remembered another curious encounter with the police that had occurred 14 years earlier, when I was travelling north on Highway 400.

"Highway 400 to Barrie was empty as I drove back to Toronto after a week of intrepid salesmanship in the small towns of southern Ontario. I was curious to see how fast my company-leased Mercury S33 Sports Sedan would go, and so I pushed down hard on the accelerator and left it there.

The long empty highway snaked down the side of a hill. In the distance, parked by the side of the road, I could see a vehicle that suspiciously looked like a police car. I knew that I was speeding, so I quickly took my foot off the accelerator. As I approached the vehicle, the car door opened, and a uniformed RCMP officer stepped out and waved me down and said,

"You were doing 190 kph in a 120 kph zone and I am going to book you for speeding. In fact, you are lucky to be only getting a ticket for that performance."

I knew that I had slowed to the legal limit before coming into range of any radar system that he might have been using. And so, I politely asked,

"Excuse me officer but how did you measure how fast I was going?"

He looked at me for a moment and then pointed first to the sky, where I saw a small plane circling overhead. Next, he pointed to the road surface stretching back up the long hill. And that was the moment when I understood the purpose of the evenly spaced broad white lines on its black asphalt surface! It was an expensive lesson, and afterwards, I always drove on Highway 400 with my side mirror pointing to the sky! "

I thought about the connection between these two events in my life, both had taken place on Highway 400 south of Barrie. It seemed an odd coincidence that the only times I have ever been warned or apprehended by traffic police, took place on the same highway: once in a car going at 190 kph and the second time, going slower on a bicycle at 15 kph!

It was now 7:30 p.m., and I was in a race with time and the setting sun. My speed was much slower, dusk was setting in, and long shadows were forming across my path. Food was forgotten, and I kept telling myself to just keep going, somehow, it would all work out. I found a phone beside a service station and called Marg to let her know my location and that I hoped to reach Richmond Hill, about 20 kilometres outside Toronto, somewhere around 10.30 p.m., where I would wait beside the road for her to find me.

Having made the call and set the stage for the ending of this long journey, I felt relaxed enough to stop and photograph my shadow on the road; surely an image that captured the experience of the moment!

A Mere Shadow 0f My Former Self

I will never forget that final ride through the rural landscape of Ontario. The gentle light of the setting sun, dark shadows lengthening in front of me. I felt at peace, the journey all but over. This ending lacked the victorious triumph of the cycling warrior that I had imagined from time to time along the way! Not the way I had planned, but I knew that I had made the right decision to end the journey in this way. To sacrifice fame and glory for the sake of love and connection; the thought did occur to me that perhaps I was not too old to learn.

I rode past the township of Newmarket as the evening light began to fade, and I still had another 20 kilometres before the meeting point with Marg at Richmond Hill. Finally, I could no longer see with my sunglasses and had to remove them. Peering into the dying light, I cycled on until I could no longer clearly see the road in front of me and was forced to dismount and push the bike.

I remember the sound of traffic speeding past me, headlights full on, briefly illuminating the night and then fading back into darkness. I trudged on, feeling tired and concerned that drivers would have difficulty seeing me on the dark shoulder of the busy highway. I had no lights on the bike, and I was not wearing safety reflectors. I had become a risk to myself and others.

And then, a car passed, slowed, and came to a stop on the side of the road ahead of me. In the light from passing vehicles, I could see three people walking toward me. It took a moment before I realized that they were Marg, Michelle, and Sean! They had found me! I was overwhelmed by love and grateful that I had survived this long and arduous journey to be with my children again.

EPILOGUE

I spent my first night at Marg's house in Toronto. We talked and laughed, told stories and were together again as a family, but we were not destined to remain together. The next morning, I packed up my gear, climbed back on the bike and cycled to the home of my friends, Jack and Susan, where I remained for the next four weeks. Eventually, I found a suitable apartment at a reasonable rent, where my children could stay with me on the weekends. And then, with a determination to succeed, a permanent tooth filling and new spectacles with clear lenses, I commenced my academic program.

I met Sandra for lunch one day in September, and we talked about our lives and the changes we were making. We were attracted to each other, but the individual challenges, that we were facing at the time, prevented the relationship from evolving further. Eventually, we lost touch and went our separate ways.

I had become extremely attached to the used bike that had carried me across Canada, even to the point of naming her "Griselda". For almost two months after my arrival in Toronto, she was my only form of transportation. I revelled in the ease and speed that she provided, as I slipped through traffic and avoided bus lineups on my way across the city. I was attached to my bike. During my long journey she had become part of my identity. I even imagined that when my riding days were over, I would hang her from a frame in the wall of my living room. And so, it was an experience of deep loss, when the dear machine was stolen and no doubt chopped up into parts by scurvy knaves, who had no idea of her true value to me.

I completed the full-time academic course requirements for a doctorate in Applied Psychology in two years. However, it took another five years to complete and defend my dissertation, during which time I was employed as a clinical counsellor in a major Toronto hospital. In 1993, complete with a doctoral degree and a title before my name, I left Toronto and returned to Vancouver, where I obtained registration as a clinical psychologist in the Province of British Columbia.

39 years have passed since I set out on that long journey from Vancouver to Toronto to be with my children. My reason for undertaking this long-distance bike ride was not to meet an athletic challenge or the desire to have an adventure but was simply transportation and the most economical way for me to get from Vancouver to Toronto at a time when I had limited funds and no income. And, although, I had underestimated the cost and amount of the food I would devour on the way, it proved to be viable form of transportation that preserved my limited cash reserves. In addition, even though conditions on various dark and stormy nights were less than ideal, I also saved a considerable amount of money by sleeping on the ground in a tent and not paying rent.

There were no cell phones or internet to connect me to the world beyond the highway or to the people that I encountered on the road. I set out with little understanding of long-distance biking at a time when such activity, particularly for older gentlemen, was not a popular thing to do. During the days and weeks of propelling myself along that endless Canadian highway, I adapted to my life on the road and gradually began to live each day as it came. I became immersed in the experience of "journey," a state of mind, of being present in the moment and not preoccupied with future and past distractions. I thought that, once I reached Toronto, "the journey" would end and I would return to being in the world and subjectively living my life as I had done before leaving Vancouver, but that did not happen.

The sense of "journey" I acquired on the road, continued after I arrived in Toronto. I returned to my children with a renewed sense of purpose and appreciation of simply being alive. Over time, I have gradually understood how deeply I was affected, psychologically, emotionally and spiritually, by that bike ride so many years ago. I do not always succeed but I am doing my best to live this journey, the journey of my life, by living in the moment, paying attention to my present experience, being connected to others and hopefully not being too preoccupied with future endings or distracted by memories of past events.

The pain of being separated from my children motivated me to cycle across Canada to be with them. During the initial stages of the journey, I felt afraid and uncertain that I would not succeed in my quest if I allowed others to get too close, and so I rode alone, and fear became my companion. I did not want to share my journey with others because I was afraid that such contact would undermine my determined resolve to continue. But people reached out to help me along the way, and I learned to trust and value their help in moments of need when I felt afraid.

There were times when I felt an intense connection to the environment, to the land itself, as I rode along day by day. Moments of emotional healing occurred for me on those long empty roads and steep hill climbs, when I cried for my father and felt connected to him in ways that were not present when he was alive.

The course and understanding of my life were changed by that long bike ride across Canada. During that journey I learned to trust an experience that for want of a better term I can only call 'love." This is not the love of romance or personal attraction, or even the form of love that the Greek philosophers called Agape but the "experience" of union; an awareness of empathic connection both to people and to the life that surrounds us in so many different forms. I have found teachers and taught myself to trust and believe in this loving awareness whenever I feel afraid, and to have faith that we are all part of something much greater than we can imagine.

STATISTICS

Total Cycling Days	44
Total Rest Days	7
Net Cycling Days	37
Total Distance	4604 Km*
Average Daily Distance	125 Km
Average Daily Speed	15 Kph
Average Hours Per Day Cycling	8.3
Average Daily Calorie Burn Rate	6000

*Kilometres To Miles

Total Distance	2860 miles
Daily Distance	77 miles
Average Speed	9.3 mph
1985 Motor Vehicle Registrations (Canada)	14.7 million
2022 Motor Vehicle Registrations (Canada)	26.3 million

BRITISH COLUMBIA to MANITOBA

VANCOUVER   BRANDON

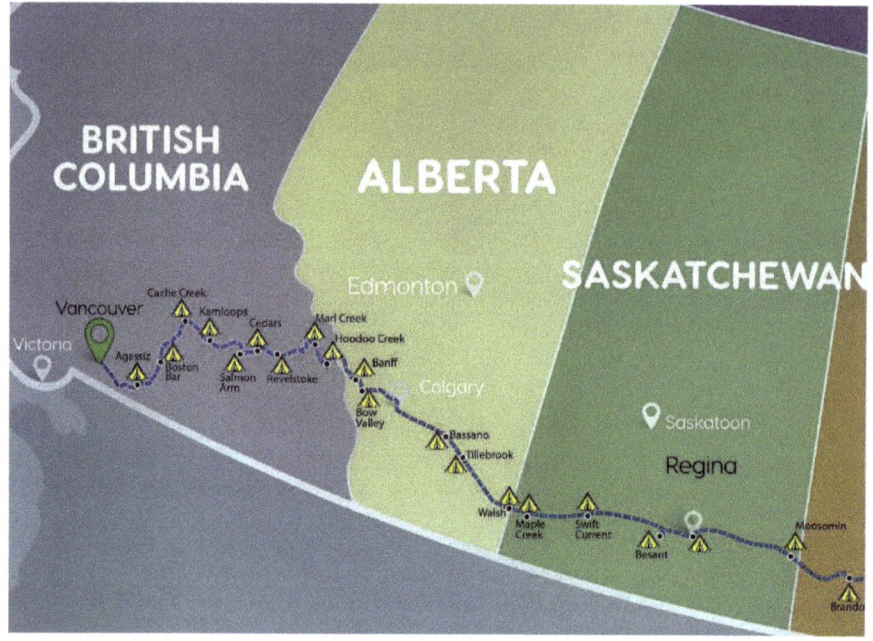

Map Credit: Sean Gilligan

DAY (1) to Day (21)

Distance Travelled 2235 Kilometres (1389 miles)

MANITOBA to ONTARIO

BRANDON   TORONTO

Map Credit: Sean Gilligan

DAY (21) to Day (44)

Distance Travelled 2369 Kilometres (1473 miles)

www.ingramcontent.com/pod-product-compliance
Lightning Source LLC
Chambersburg PA
CBHW041141110526
44590CB00027B/4094